Parliaments and Post-Legislative Scrutiny

To what extent have parliaments a responsibility to monitor how laws are implemented as intended and have the expected impact? Is the practice of Post-Legislative Scrutiny emerging as a new dimension within the oversight role of parliament? What approach do parliaments apply in assessing the implementation and impact of legislation? These are the fascinating questions guiding this book.

Case studies offer an in-depth look at how particular countries and the European Union conduct Post-Legislative Scrutiny. The analysis puts Post-Legislative Scrutiny in the context of parliamentary oversight and parliaments' engagement in the legislative cycle.

The purpose of this book is to demonstrate the value of Post-Legislative Scrutiny as a public good, benefiting the executive, legislature and the people in ensuring that law delivers what is expected of it, as well as to respond to the need for greater clarity as to what is meant by the term. In this way, the publication can assist legislatures to think more clearly as to what precisely they understand, and seek to achieve, by Post-Legislative Scrutiny.

This book is the result of the co-operation between the Centre for Legislative Studies at the University of Hull and the Westminster Foundation for Democracy.

The chapters were originally published as a special issue of *The Journal of Legislative Studies*.

Franklin De Vrieze is Senior Governance Adviser at Westminster Foundation for Democracy. He specializes in Post-Legislative Scrutiny and legislative processes, financial accountability in governance and anti-corruption.

Philip Norton is Professor of Government at the University of Hull, UK, and sits in the UK House of Lords as Lord Norton of Louth. He was the first Chair of the House of Lords Constitution Committee.

Library of Legislative Studies
Series Editor: Lord Philip Norton of Louth, University of Hull, UK

Parliaments and Citizens
Edited by Cristina Leston-Bandeira

Legislatures of Small States
A Comparative Study
Edited by Nicholas D. J. Baldwin

Parliamentary Communication in EU Affairs
Connecting with the Electorate?
Edited by Katrin Auel and Tapio Raunio

Government-Opposition in Southern European Countries during the Economic Crisis
Great Recession, Great Cooperation?
Edited by Elisabetta De Giorgi and Catherine Moury

The Legislature of Brazil
An Analysis of Its Policy-making and Public Engagement Roles
Edited by Cristiane Brum Bernardes, Cristina Leston-Bandeira and Ricardo de João Braga

Regional Parliaments
Effective Actors in EU Policy-Making?
Edited by Gabriele Abels and Anna-Lena Hogenauer

The Iberian Legislatures in Comparative Perspective
Edited by Jorge M. Fernandes and Cristina Leston-Bandeira

The Impact of Legislatures
A Quarter-Century of The Journal of Legislative Studies
Edited by Philip Norton

Parliaments and Post-Legislative Scrutiny
Edited by Franklin De Vrieze and Philip Norton

This volume on post-legislative scrutiny is the result of the co-operation between the Centre for Legislative Studies at the University of Hull and the Westminster Foundation for Democracy (WFD). It draws primarily, though not exclusively, on papers delivered initially at three conferences. These were the University of Hull and WFD expert seminar on legislative impact assessments in April 2019, the ECPR Standing Group on Parliaments meeting in June 2019 and the 14th Workshop of Parliamentary Scholars and Parliamentarians held at Wroxton College, Oxfordshire in the UK, in July 2019. Those selected for inclusion have subsequently been revised in the light of feedback from the conferences as well as being peer-reviewed.

Parliaments and Post-Legislative Scrutiny

Edited by
Franklin De Vrieze and Philip Norton

LONDON AND NEW YORK

First published 2021
by Routledge
2 Park Square, Milton Park, Abingdon, Oxon, OX14 4RN

and by Routledge
52 Vanderbilt Avenue, New York, NY 10017

Routledge is an imprint of the Taylor & Francis Group, an informa business

© 2021 Taylor & Francis

All rights reserved. No part of this book may be reprinted or reproduced or utilised in any form or by any electronic, mechanical, or other means, now known or hereafter invented, including photocopying and recording, or in any information storage or retrieval system, without permission in writing from the publishers.

Trademark notice: Product or corporate names may be trademarks or registered trademarks, and are used only for identification and explanation without intent to infringe.

British Library Cataloguing-in-Publication Data
A catalogue record for this book is available from the British Library

ISBN13: 978-0-367-67756-5

Typeset in Minion Pro
by codeMantra

Publisher's Note
The publisher accepts responsibility for any inconsistencies that may have arisen during the conversion of this book from journal articles to book chapters, namely the inclusion of journal terminology.

Disclaimer
Every effort has been made to contact copyright holders for their permission to reprint material in this book. The publishers would be grateful to hear from any copyright holder who is not here acknowledged and will undertake to rectify any errors or omissions in future editions of this book.

Printed in the United Kingdom
by Henry Ling Limited

Contents

	Citation Information	viii
	Notes on Contributors	x
1	The significance of post-legislative scrutiny *Franklin De Vrieze and Philip Norton*	1
2	A deliberative approach to post legislative scrutiny? Lessons from Australia's ad hoc approach *Sarah Moulds*	14
3	The UK post-legislative scrutiny gap *Tom Caygill*	39
4	Ex-post evaluation in the European Parliament: an increasing influence on the policy cycle *Irmgard Anglmayer and Amandine Scherrer*	57
5	Post-Legislative Scrutiny in Europe: how the oversight on implementation of legislation by parliaments in Europe is getting stronger *Franklin De Vrieze*	79
6	How parliaments monitor sustainable development goals – a ground for application of post legislative scrutiny *Fotios Fitsilis and Franklin De Vrieze*	100
7	Towards parliamentary full cycle engagement in the legislative process: innovations and challenges *Jonathan Murphy*	121
	Index	147

Citation Information

The chapters in this book were originally published in *The Journal of Legislative Studies*, volume 26, issue 3 (July 2020). When citing this material, please use the original page numbering for each article, as follows:

Chapter 1
The significance of post-legislative scrutiny
Franklin De Vrieze and Philip Norton
The Journal of Legislative Studies, volume 26, issue 3 (July 2020) pp. 349–361

Chapter 2
A deliberative approach to post legislative scrutiny? Lessons from Australia's ad hoc approach
Sarah Moulds
The Journal of Legislative Studies, volume 26, issue 3 (July 2020) pp. 362–386

Chapter 3
The UK post-legislative scrutiny gap
Tom Caygill
The Journal of Legislative Studies, volume 26, issue 3 (July 2020) pp. 387–404

Chapter 4
Ex-post evaluation in the European Parliament: an increasing influence on the policy cycle
Irmgard Anglmayer and Amandine Scherrer
The Journal of Legislative Studies, volume 26, issue 3 (July 2020) pp. 405–426

Chapter 5
Post-Legislative Scrutiny in Europe: how the oversight on implementation of legislation by parliaments in Europe is getting stronger
Franklin De Vrieze
The Journal of Legislative Studies, volume 26, issue 3 (July 2020) pp. 427–447

Chapter 6
How parliaments monitor sustainable development goals – a ground for application of post legislative scrutiny
Fotios Fitsilis and Franklin De Vrieze
The Journal of Legislative Studies, volume 26, issue 3 (July 2020) pp. 448–468

Chapter 7
Towards parliamentary full cycle engagement in the legislative process: innovations and challenges
Jonathan Murphy
The Journal of Legislative Studies, volume 26, issue 3 (July 2020) pp. 469–493

For any permission-related enquiries please visit:
http://www.tandfonline.com/page/help/permissions

Contributors

Irmgard Anglmayer is policy analyst in the European Parliamentary Research Service (EPRS), the internal research service and think-tank of the European Parliament.

Tom Caygill is Lecturer in politics in the School of Geography, Politics and Sociology at Newcastle University, UK.

Franklin De Vrieze is Senior Governance Adviser at Westminster Foundation for Democracy. He specializes in Post-Legislative Scrutiny and legislative processes, financial accountability in governance and anti-corruption.

Fotios Fitsilis has academic background in Law, Economics and Engineering. Since 2008, he is a researcher at the Scientific Service of the Hellenic Parliament. He has been Visiting Professor at the Universidad Complutense de Madrid, Spain.

Sarah Moulds is Lecturer at the University of South Australia's Law School, Australia. She has teaching and research interests in the area of public law, human rights, counterterrorism and criminal law, administrative law and anti-discrimination law.

Jonathan Murphy manages INTER PARES, an EU-funded global parliamentary strengthening programme delivered by International IDEA, Stockholm, Sweden. He is currently Docent (Visiting Professor) at the University of Jyväskylä, Finland.

Philip Norton is Professor of Government at the University of Hull, UK, and sits in the House of Lords as Lord Norton of Louth. He was the first Chair of the House of Lords Constitution Committee.

Amandine Scherrer, formerly policy analyst in the European Parliamentary Research Service, works as policy expert at the European Banking Authority (EBA) in Paris.

The significance of post-legislative scrutiny
Franklin De Vrieze and Philip Norton

A legislature is a core institution of the state. Its core defining function is that of giving assent to measures of public policy that are to be binding (Norton, 1990, p. 1). The process by which a measure becomes a law has four principal stages: gestation, drafting, deliberation and adoption, and implementation (see Norton, 2013, pp. 70-7) The legislature is principally and necessarily core to the third stage. Prior to giving assent to a measure, it will normally debate its merits. In some legislatures, primarily in non-democratic nations, the debate may be perfunctory or formal. In others, it may be extensive and measures may be amended, sometimes rejected, as a result of the deliberations.

Legislatures have been studied since one can identify them as having come into being, but over the past century scholarly study has been both limited and narrow. It has been limited because of the perception that, as Lord Bryce notably argued, legislatures are in decline (Bryce, 1921, pp. 367-77). Power, he argued, had departed legislatures and gone elsewhere. Mass membership political parties, operating in an era of an expanding franchise, ensured executive dominance of the legislature and the approval of its measures. The focus of study thus shifted elsewhere, not least to executives and bureaucracies. When legislatures were studied, not least those legislatures that did exert some capacity to allocate values (most notably the US Congress), the focus was what happened in the legislature during the passage of a measure. When in post-war years there was a shift in study in the US to behavioural analysis, there was a focus on how members operated within the legislature in determining the outcome of legislation.

Recent years, especially since the 1980s, have seen a shift in scholarly attention to legislatures (Martin et al., 2014; Norton, 2020) with some groundbreaking research, not least in the USA. As Martin, Saalfeld and Strom observed, there was a shift from the macro-level analyses of 'old' institutionalism to a micro level of analysis, inspired by a general rise of behaviouralism in the social sciences. 'In this conception of a political system the formal institutions of government were reduced to the "black box", where the conversion of inputs into outputs occurred' (Martin et al., 2014, p. 9). There were analyses of how members saw their roles and how they were shaped by the political environment in which they operated. Members of the legislature did not exist in a vacuum, but the focus was the influences on members during the deliberative stage of the policy process. Other than in the USA, an outlier in terms of its capacity to shape measures independently of the executive, there has been little attention given to the input side of legislation – the gestation and drafting stages of bills – and to the output side in terms of the implementation of measures.

That this should be so is not surprising. Executive bills are laid before the legislature – they have been prepared by the executive – and once approved the measures are then implemented by the executive and other public agencies. Any dispute as to meaning is a matter for the courts. The initiation stage of the policy process is dominated typically by political parties, executive bodies and by organised interests. The drafting stage is dominated by the executive, which may utilise lawyers specialised in drawing up bills, as in the Office of Parliamentary Counsel in the UK and the Office of Management and Budget in the USA. The output side of the process is dominated by bodies at whom the legislation is directed or by bodies, such as the police, responsible for law enforcement. Any dispute as to the meaning of the law is, as mentioned, a matter usually for resolution in the courts.

There has thus been a significant growth in the study of legislatures, both quantitatively and qualitatively, but the focus has been the stage of deliberation and assent by the legislature. It reflects how legislatures how generally acted, devoting their resources to deliberations on bills once introduced. For legislatures, the beginning of the legislative process is when a bill is introduced and it ends when it is approved and becomes law.

The UK serves as an exemplar of this perception. The executive introduces a bill fully drafted, drawn up by the Office of Parliamentary Counsel acting on instructions from the relevant Government department. The minister in charge may negotiate with others, including organised interests and ministerial colleagues, to gain approval prior to the introduction of the bill. The legislature is not among the bodies that are involved (Norton, 2013, pp. 74–5), although anticipation of parliamentary reaction may shape how the bill is drawn up in order to smooth its passage through both Houses (Norton, 2019, p. 342). For ministers, and for backbench Members of Parliament, legislative success is seen as the bill receiving Royal Assent and becoming an Act of Parliament. In short, for a minister, the measure of success is essentially getting their bills enacted rather than whether the measures achieve their desired goals.

Recent years have seen a change in how some legislatures view the legislative process. This has led to a change in structures and processes, one that as we shall see has been rather disparate in both form and effect. As a result of this development, there is a growing body of scholarly analysis of these changes. This volume is a contribution to that analysis. It focuses on one particular dimension: post-legislative scrutiny.

Taking A holistic view

In 2004, the Constitution Committee of the House of Lords (chaired by Philip Norton) published a report entitled *Parliament and the Legislative Process* (Constitution Committee, 2004). The committee was not the first to examine the case for some review of legislation once it was on the statute book (Hansard Society, 1993; Procedure Committee, 1990). It was distinctive, though, for two reasons: first, for taking a holistic view of the process by which law was made and enacted and, second, for its consequences. It triggered a significant series of events.

The committee considered both the input as well as output side of legislation, examining whether Parliament could play a role in both the drafting and the implementation stages, as well as considering how both Houses could be strengthened in scrutinising and influencing bills once they had been introduced. It was keen to see an extension of a practice that had begun in 1997 of some bills being sent for consideration by a parliamentary committee before being formally introduced to Parliament. This practice enabled parliamentarians to comment and potentially influence the drafting a bill before the Government had committed itself to the contents. However, only a minority of bills was sent for pre-legislative scrutiny. The committee favoured pr-legislative scrutiny being the norm rather than the exception (Constitution Committee, 2004, pp. 43–4). However, it was its recommendations on post-legislative scrutiny that were to have the most notable effect.

The committee was conscious that little attention was given by Parliament to measures once enacted. There were reviews of Acts by parliamentary committees when the measures had demonstrably had notably visible and unintended consequences, but such reviews were rare. There was no systematic scrutiny and parliamentary committees accorded no priority to it. The committee advanced a case for post-legislative scrutiny – we shall return to the justifications for such scrutiny – and recommended that post-legislative scrutiny be routine, with Acts being reviewed within three years of their commencement or six years after enactment, whichever was the sooner (Constitution Committee, 2004, p. 44).

As the committee recognised, there was widespread agreement as to the principle of post-legislative scrutiny. The problem was getting agreement to its implementation. Nothing had happened when previous bodies had recommended it. In its response to the committee's report, the government acknowledged the value of post-legislative scrutiny (Constitution Committee, 2005, p. 9), but demurred from acting to implement the recommendations. Instead, contending that the term was ill-defined, it referred the matter to the Law Commission (an official body headed by a judge, set up to consider law reform) to examine options and to consider what body may be most suitable for the role.

In its report the following year, the Commission endorsed the Constitution Committee recommendation for systematic post-legislative scrutiny – for which it had found 'overwhelming support' – and for the appointment of a joint committee of both Houses on post-legislative scrutiny (Law Commission, 2006, p. 5). The government took two years to respond, but when it did it concurred in the commission's overall approach, but adopted a different scheme of scrutiny. It agreed that most Acts, three to five years after enactment, would be reviewed by the relevant government department, with the reviews published as command papers and sent to the appropriate departmental select committee in the House of Commons (Leader of the House of Commons, 2008, pp. 20–22). It was then up to the relevant committee if it wished to further examine the Act.

Our concern here is not with the extent to which post-legislative scrutiny has been undertaken, and with what effect, in the UK Parliament. That has been the subject of examination elsewhere (Caygill, 2019a, 2019b; Norton, 2019) as well as in this volume by Caygill. The picture has clearly been patchy. Our concern here is with the formal recognition of the importance of post-legislative scrutiny and how it has since expanded and been taken up by legislatures around the globe. As Sarah Moulds notes in her analysis of the Australian experience of post-legislative scrutiny, what happened in the UK influenced other nations, not least with a Westminster heritage or receiving development assistance from UK donors or aid agencies.

Assessing post-Legislative scrutiny

There are three key questions to be asked about post-legislative scrutiny. *First*, what is it? What exactly does it encompass? *Second*, who does it? Is it essentially a formal exercise to be undertaken by specialists, or a process to be undertaken by those who enacted the measure and who are able to hold government to account for how it has been implemented? Addressing the who also touches upon the how, be it by committee or some other agency. And, *third*, *why* do it? Given the demands made of legislatures and other public bodies, why should potentially scare resources be devoted to it? Here, we provide a brief summary in preparation for what follows in this volume. Mould in her analysis goes into greater detail.

What is it?

Post-legislative scrutiny has been defined in different ways in different jurisdictions. Furthermore, in some cases it is carried out, but without being styled as post-legislative scrutiny. The term itself is only now beginning to gain some currency, but the recognition, as we shall see illustrated in this issue, is not universal. It has also been extended beyond what both the House of Lords Constitution Committee and UK Law Commission meant by the term. Indeed, it has become something of an elastic term, the elasticity extending to both components of the term – scrutiny and legislation.

In terms of the *scrutiny*, we can identify two purposes. One is an evaluative role, that is, seeking to that ensure the normative aims of policies are reflected in the effects of legislation, in other words to assess whether a piece of legislation has been implemented effectively and achieved its intended aims. This was how the Constitution Committee interpreted the term. It favoured government, when bringing forward a bill, to identify the criteria by which one would know whether it had achieved its purpose as a means of aiding objective, rather than partisan, scrutiny of the effect of the Act. It was also the interpretation adopted by the Law Commission. This is primarily what we understand by the term scrutiny. Though it may encompass seeking to be objective, or at least non-partisan, it is essentially a political role.

However, some legislatures have interpreted the term in more a legal, or formalistic, manner, treating PLS as a monitoring function, examining the application of legislation and the adoption of the necessary secondary legislation to give effect to it. In several countries, there is the risk that laws are voted for but not applied, that associated secondary legislation is not adopted, or that there is insufficient information on the actual state of a law's implementation and its effects (De Vrieze, 2019a). Implementation does not happen automatically and several incidents can affect its course including changes in facts on the ground, diversion of resources, deflection of goals, resistance from stakeholders and changes in the legal framework of related policy fields (De Vrieze, 2018). In such systems, there is a case for ensuring that the law has been given effect.

We thus have a distinction between the interpretative and the formalistic (De Vrieze & Hasson, 2017; Karpen, 2009; Kelly & Everett, 2013; Norton, 2019). The two are not mutually exclusive, but the extension of the term to encompass a formalistic role of oversight means that we need to be clear as to which interpretation is being adopted. Given now common usage of the term post-legislative scrutiny to encompass both, we retain PLS as the generic term. However, we consider that there may be a case, as we go forward, for adopting greater rigour and using PLS solely for scrutiny – that is the evaluative function – and post-legislative oversight (PLO) for the more legal, or formalistic, function. The distinction may have practical as well as intellectual value. It may encourage some legislatures to move beyond a formalistic, or tick-box, exercise to engage more directly with evaluating the consequences of measures that they have enacted.

In terms of the *legislation* being scrutinised, the Constitution Committee and the Law Commission meant legislation enacted by the UK national legislature. It was the legislature examining whether the measures it had passed had delivered on what was expected of them. Legislatures may be engaging in scrutiny, but for it to be post-legislative, there has to be legislation in the first place. However, the term has since been expanded by some commentators to encompass goals set not by the legislature, but by other bodies. This has been notably the case with sustainable development goals (SDGs), established by the United Nations, as discussed by Fitsilis and De Vrieze in their contribution to the volume. Some SDGs may be delivered through legislatures enacting primary and secondary legislation, but others are met independently of any domestic legislation. As Fitsilis and De Vrieze note, the Inter-Parliamentary Union (IPU) has an especially important role in utilising field missions to engage with parliaments to assess their capacity to integrate SDGs via dedicated legislation. Where there is such legislation, then scrutinising it once enacted to see if it has achieved its purpose falls within post-legislative scrutiny. Their article raises the question of how and to what extent the concept can be applied to goals set externally. Should one draw on the concept as a guide to systematic scrutiny, but utilise a modified or different term?

Who does it?

Where it is undertaken, the task of engaging in post-legislative scrutiny, or oversight, varies from nation to nation, not unrelated to the different interpretations. The legal, or formalistic, approach is something more easily undertaken by officials, whereas the evaluative, or political, approach is one more appropriately undertaken by legislators.

As Jonathan Murphy records in his study, there are different ways of carrying out post-legislative scrutiny. Practice varies considerably, as is clear from the contributions to this volume. Parliaments may utilise committees, commissions, external working bodies, or independent state agencies. Parliamentary committees offer the most direct form of engagement. As Fitsilis and De Vrieze point out in their article, in some parliaments, it is the Legal or Legislative Committee that conducts the review of the enactment of legislation, while the thematic committees evaluate whether the laws have achieved their purpose. In some cases, the remit for PLS is explicitly assigned to a dedicated committee, as is the case in the Scottish and Lebanese parliaments. The more formalistic form of PLS may be undertaken by a range of bodies, be it official agencies independent of the legislature or by bodies appointed by and answerable to the legislature.

There is also the distinction to be drawn between conferring the task on someone and that task being undertaken. There are resource implications to undertaking PLS as well as an opportunity cost. Why should legislators engage in post-legislative scrutiny if there is more political advantage in focusing on scrutinising bills as they pass through the legislature? Partisan theory is most powerful for explaining most committee activity in legislatures (Cox & McCubbins, 1993). There is not much partisan advantage to appointing committees to engage in post-legislative scrutiny. There may thus be limited incentives to engage in such activity.

The problem is illustrated well in the case of the UK Parliament. Both Houses engage in some degree of post-legislative scrutiny. However, the form varies between the chambers. As Norton has argued elsewhere, distributive and informational theories serve to explain the differences (Norton, 2019, p. 347). In the House of Commons, the driver for undertaking post-legislative scrutiny by committee is the committee members. In the House of Lords, it is the chamber. There are thus differences in form. There are also differences in application. In the House of Commons, scrutiny is sporadic. In the House of Lords, it is limited but consistent. However, in both, it is not extensive. There is, as Tom Caygill identifies in his article, a post-legislative gap in the UK. Though government departments review Acts three to five years after enactment, neither House utilises these as the basis for regular post-legislative scrutiny. The nature of incentive is one that is clearly crucial.

Why do it?

Why do legislatures engage in post-legislative scrutiny? Since the development of the term, PLS has become a notable feature in some legislatures. It is now receiving recognition, and scholarly attention, on a growing scale. Some scholarship has been substantial, not least Caygill's PhD thesis on the subject (Caygill, 2019a). More articles are now starting to appear. It was the subject of a special issue of the *European Journal of Law Reform* in 2019. The Westminster Foundation for Democracy (WFD) has been especially active in generating analyses and reports. But what is the rationale for the activity?

Post-legislative scrutiny may be seen as a public good. The principal justifications for undertaking it were advanced by the Constitution Committee in its 2004 report as improving the quality of law and of government.

"Regular scrutiny will determine if Acts have done what they were intended to achieve; if not, it may then be possible to identify alternative means of achieving those goals. Scrutiny may also have the effect of ensuring that those who are meant to be implementing the measures are, in fact, implementing them in the way intended.

Such scrutiny may also impose a much greater discipline on Government. We have already touched upon the fact that Ministers often see achievement in terms of getting their 'big bill' on the statute book. They may engage in greater circumspection if they knew that in future the measure of their success was not so much getting a measure on the statute book as the effect that it had.

As such, post-legislative scrutiny may improve the quality of Government. It may also contribute to improvement in the legislative process ... We have stressed throughout this report the importance of ensuring that Parliament has mechanisms to ensure that bills are fit for purpose, but how does Parliament know that the bills, once enacted, have actually proved fit for purpose?" (Constitution Committee, 2004, pp. 42–3).

In addition, one can mention the need to act preventively regarding potential adverse effects of new legislation on fundamental rights, as well as, for instance, on the environment or on economic and social welfare (Fitsilis & De Vrieze, 2019).

The growing impetus for PLS coincides with the rationalisation of the law-making process, and a growing demand for the quality of legislation to be reviewed as well as procedures that can support parliaments to manage contemporary 'legislative complexity' (Heaton, 2013). PLS is an effort to support this by institutionalising and systematising a moment of analysis and assessment focusing specifically on improving the quality of legislation passed. As such it should improve a parliament's understanding of the causal relations between a law and its effects as the accuracy of assumptions underlying legislation are tested after its enactment (Karpen, 2009). PLS as a form of legislative evaluation is therefore a learning process that both contributes to a parliament's knowledge of the impacts of legislation but also its know-how in ensuring legislation meets the needs of relevant stakeholders. By implication, PLS may reduce ambiguity and distrust and allows the legislator to learn by doing (De Vrieze, 2019b).

The act of carrying out PLS can therefore be justified as a stand-alone activity that enables a parliament to self-monitor and evaluate, as well as reflect on the merits of its own democratic output and internal technical ability. Various parliaments, a variety of which are discussed in this volume, are beginning to institutionalise PLS as a separate mechanism within parliament (Norton, 2019).

While PLS can take the form of a separate mechanism within parliament, the process of evaluation is also the by-product of a parliament carrying out effective executive oversight, assessing the extent to which a government is managing the effective implementation of its policies and abiding by statutory obligations. As indicated in the Constitution Committee's report, the existence of PLS may also serve to focus the minds of the drafters of legislation on the impact of legislation and not solely on ensuring that it is drafted in a way that will ensure that it is passed. In the UK, bills have been drafted to get through Parliament. 'That', as one leading judge observed, 'is the draftsman's principal task' (Lord Rodger of Earlsferry, quoted in Norton, 2019, p. 342). Knowing that a measure may be subject to post-legislative review may encourage those responsible for drawing up bills to raise their sights beyond the assent stage and consider more those at whom the measure is directed.

However, the act of carrying out PLS on a primary basis is also one that extends beyond executive oversight, as an internal monitoring and evaluation system by which a parliament is also able to consider and reflect on the merits of its own democratic output and internal technical ability. Seen in this way, PLS also provides an approach that a parliament may take to its legislative role as one that is not only the maker of laws but also a country's legislative watchdog.

It is also possible to identify a third justification for post-legislative scrutiny. That is, encouraging citizens to engage more with the parliament. This is the consequence, or potential consequence, advanced by Moulds in her study of ad hoc experience in Australia. It is also a potential consequence touched upon by Fitsilis and De Vrieze in their study of evaluating delivery of sustainable development goals and by Murphy in looking at full-cycle engagement by parliaments in the legislative engagement.

Moulds identifies community-initiated PLS as one of four trigger points for scrutiny, contending that it has the potential to be highly deliberative in nature and provide the basis for experimenting with less conventional forms of parliamentary-community engagement. She illustrates the impact of community initiative and engagement through two case studies, the post-legislative review of the Sex Discrimination Act – encouraged by civic prompting and influenced in content by community engagement – and of the Marriage Act. As she recognises, the latter case study in particular illustrates the problem of determining what does and does not constitute post-legislative scrutiny. Post-legislative scrutiny is not necessarily a purely self-contained activity, but – as in the Australian review of the Marriage Act illustrates – constitute part of a wider process of initiating change.

Limitations

Although an activity may be desirable in principle, there may be problems in its execution. The UK Law Commission made three cautionary comments about PLS, which highlight its limitations:

(1) *Risk of replay of arguments.* As the Commission recognised, PLS should concentrate on the outcomes of legislation. Unless self-discipline is exercised by the reviewing body, and those giving evidence to it, there is a danger of it degenerating into a replay of arguments advanced during the passage of the Bill. The criteria for determining whether a measure has achieved its purpose needs to be clear in advance in order to avoid a repeat of the debate on principle. The important consideration is that it is a review and not a replay.

(2) *Dependence on political will.* As we have noted, PLS may be desirable, but it may not be achievable if the political will to deliver it is missing. It is possible to come up with an ideal scheme for reforming a political system, but it requires action on the part of those who are necessary to implement it (see Norton, 1983, pp. 54–69). Identifying the end point is necessary (there needs to be a clear goal), but it is not sufficient. The evolution of a more systematic approach to PLS will depend on a combination of political will and political judgment. Ensuring law does what it is designed to do is a public good and drafters giving greater thought to the effect, and not simply the passage, of legislation may enhance government and legislative efficiency in terms of avoiding the need for time and resource consuming amending legislation. However, both the legislature and the executive need to have the confidence to recognise that and commit to implementing regular post-legislative scrutiny.

(3) *Resource constraints.* PLS, as we have noted, places demands on resources and time available. It carries a cost not only in time and expenditure on the part of the legislature, but also on the part of those called on to provide evidence. Consultation with key stakeholders is generally necessary if relevant data are to be obtained and an accurate evaluation of effectiveness is to be made. In these circumstances, it is usually beyond the capacity of parliaments to conduct a systematic evaluation of *entire* legislative schemes. Nonetheless, the results of evaluations by government departments (as in the UK) or official bodies (as in Australia) can provide the basis upon which parliamentarians can question and hold to account those responsible for the policy and its implementation. This is based on the evaluations being made public, in itself essential to ensuring accountability (De Vrieze, 2019b).

We would add a fourth limitation. Just as Royal Assent to an Act should not be seen as the end of a process, neither should completion of post-legislative scrutiny of an Act. PLS is a means to an end rather than an end in itself. It needs to be locked into the wider parliamentary process, amenable to debate and, as appropriate, further action considered to address any problems identified with the legislation. It needs also to be widely disseminated in order to engage community interest and ensure wide accountability. However, ensuring it is not an end in itself brings us back to political will. Both parliaments and executives have to recognise it is in their interests to ensure that law does what they intended it to do.

This volume

This volume on post-legislative scrutiny is the result of the co-operation between the Centre for Legislative Studies at the University of Hull and the

Westminster Foundation for Democracy (WFD). It draws primarily, though not exclusively, on papers delivered initially at three conferences. These were the University of Hull and WFD expert seminar on legislative impact assessments in April 2019, the ECPR Standing Group on Parliaments meeting in June 2019 and the 14th Workshop of Parliamentary Scholars and Parliamentarians held at Wroxton College, Oxfordshire in the UK, in July 2019. Those selected for inclusion have subsequently been revised in the light of feedback from the conferences as well as being peer-reviewed.

Each article is included as a free-standing contribution in order to ensure its intellectual integrity. This approach also has particular utility in terms of what we seek to achieve. That is, it emphasises the extent to which the concept of post-legislative scrutiny remains fluid. Authors discuss their understanding of the concept. There is some notable overlap, but also differences of conceptualisation and emphasis. We treat these as demonstrating the case for seeking to resolve what is meant by post-legislative scrutiny. We have sought here to identify the problem, rather than solving it. This volume is offered as a starting point in the exercise, not an end point.

The contributions are essentially grouped thematically, starting with a series of case studies addressing post-legislative scrutiny, looking in depth at particular countries and the European Union, and then studies that take us beyond scrutiny to oversight and concluding with two that put the debate in a broader context. The grouping provides a basic framework, while the range demonstrates that the term post-legislative scrutiny is neither uniformly employed, nor its meaning interpreted in the same way. They help demonstrate the current elasticity of the term and the extent to which it may extend beyond scrutiny as well as beyond legislation enacted by the legislature.

The final paper, by Jonathan Murphy, puts the value of post-legislative scrutiny in a wider systemic context, ensuring we do not see it as a discrete development in seeking to improve parliaments' engagement in the legislative process. In many respects, Murphy's article brings the analysis full circle. The House of Lords Constitution Committee looked at the legislative process holistically, seeing delivery of post-legislative scrutiny as an integral part of a wider process of change to enhance the UK Parliament's role in enhancing the quality of law in the United Kingdom. Murphy locates post-legislative scrutiny similarly in a wider full-cycle process of parliamentary engagement in the legislative process.

The purpose of this collection therefore is to demonstrate the value of post-legislative scrutiny – a public good, benefiting the executive, legislature and the people in ensuring law delivers what is expected of it – as well as the need for greater clarity as to what is meant by the term. Achieving that is not only necessary for the purposes of intellectual rigour, but also has practical application in getting legislatures to think more clearly as to what precisely they understand, and seek to achieve, by post-legislative scrutiny.

Disclosure statement

No potential conflict of interest was reported by the author(s).

ORCID

Franklin De Vrieze http://orcid.org/0000-0001-5054-1313

References

Bryce, L. (1921). *Modern Democracies*, Vol. II. Macmillan.
Caygill, T. (2019a). *A critical analysis of post-legisative scrutiny in the UK Parliament* [Doctoral dissertation]. University of Newcastle-Upon-Tyne, Newcastle-Upon-Tyne. https://theses.ncl.ac.uk/jspui/handle/10443/4626
Caygill, T. (2019b). A tale of two houses. *European Journal of Law Reform, 2*, 87–101. https://doi.org/10.5553/EJLR/138723702019021002002
Constitution Committee, House of Lords. (2004). *Parliament and the Legislative Process*, 14th Report, Session 2003-04, HL Paper 173-I.
Constitution Committee, House of Lords. (2005). *Parliament and the Legislative Process: Government's Response*, Session 2004-05, HL Paper 114.
Cox, G. W., & McCubbins, M. D. (1993). *Legislative Leviathan: Party government in the House*. Cambridge University Press.
De Vrieze, F. (2018). Principles of Post-Legislative Scrutiny by Parliaments. Retrieved October 10, 2019, from https://www.wfd.org/2018/07/23/principles-of-post-legislative-scrutiny/
De Vrieze, F. (2019a). Engaging parliaments on reviewing legislative impact. Retrieved October 10, 2019, from https://parliamentsandlegislatures.wordpress.com/2019/05/08/parliaments-post-legislative-scrutiny/
De Vrieze, F. (2019b). Introduction to post-legislative scrutiny. *European Journal of Law Reform, 21*(2), 84–86. https://doi.org/10.5553/EJLR/138723702019021002001
De Vrieze, F., & Hasson, V. (2017). *Post-legislative scrutiny*. Westminster Foundation for Democracy.
Fitsilis, F., & De Vrieze, F. (2019, June). *How Parliaments Monitor Sustainable Development Goals - A Ground for Application of Post Legislative Scrutiny* [Paper presented]. the Academic Seminar on Post-Legislative Scrutiny in Asia, Westminster Foundation for Democracy, Yangon.
Hansard Society. (1993). *The report of the Hansard Society commission on the legislative process*.
Heaton, R. (2013). When laws become Too Complex. A review into the causes of complex legislation. In *Office of the parliamentary Counsel*. Office of Parliamentary

Counsel. https://assets.publishing.service.gov.uk/government/uploads/system/uploads/attachment_data/file/187015/GoodLaw_report_8April_AP.pdf

Karpen, U. (2009). Good Governance through Transparent application of the Rule of Law. *European Journal of Law Reform*, *11*(2).

Kelly, R., & Everett, M. (2013). Post-Legislative Scrutiny. House of Commons Library, SN/PC/05232. Retrieved October 10, 2019, from https://researchbriefings.parliament.uk/ResearchBriefing/Summary/SN05232

Law Commission. (2006). *Post-Legislative Scrutiny*, Law Com No 302, Cm 6945. Retrieved October 10, 2019, from http://www.lawcom.gov.uk/app/uploads/2015/03/lc302_Post-legislative_Scrutiny.pdf

Leader of the House of Commons. (2008). *Post-legislative scrutiny – the government's approach*, Cm 7320.

Martin, S., Saalfeld, T., & Strom, K. W. (2014). Introduction. In S. Martin, T. Saalfeld, & K. W. Strom (Eds.), *The Oxford Handbook of legislative studies* (pp. 1–25). Oxford University Press.

Norton, P. (1983). The Norton view. In D. Judge (Ed.), *The Politics of parliamentary reform* (pp. 54–69). Heinemann Educational Books.

Norton, P. (1990). General introduction. In P. Norton (Ed.), *Legislatures* (pp. 1–16). Oxford University Press.

Norton, P. (2013). *Parliament in British Politics* (2nd ed.). Palgrave Macmillan.

Norton, P. (2019). Post-Legislative scrutiny in the UK Parliament: Adding value. *The Journal of Legislative Studies*, *25*(3), 340–357. https://doi.org/10.1080/13572334.2019.1633778

Norton, P. (2020). Introduction: A Quarter-century of scholarship. In P. Norton (Ed.), *The impact of legislatures* (pp. 1–11). Routledge.

Procedure Committee, House of Commons. (1990). *The Working of the Select Committee System*. 2nd Report, Session 1989-90, HC 19-I.

A deliberative approach to post legislative scrutiny? Lessons from Australia's ad hoc approach

Sarah Moulds

ABSTRACT

The elusive concept of post legislative scrutiny (PLS) is slowly starting to capture the attention of Westminster inspired Parliaments around the world with its promise of improving the implementation and quality of law making through systematic review, with benefits of the citizen on the ground. Assumptions are made within the idea of PLS about who should be responsible for the scrutiny (the Parliament) and how it should occur in practice (often led and supported by Executive agencies). However, in many jurisdictions, including Australia, the term 'PLS' is not well known because the act of post-legislative scrutiny occurs on an ad hoc basis, without any clear systematic or prescribed framework for monitoring how, when or why it might occur. This gives rise to concerns that the quality of PLS occurring in jurisdictions like Australia might be lacking and demands for a more structured approach. This article shares these concerns but argues that the experience of PLS in Australia offers important insights how to invest PLS systems with the type of deliberative features that are necessary to ensure that scrutiny of implementation and lawmaking delivers meaningful outcomes for citizens on the ground.

Part 1: introduction and key concepts

The elusive concept of post legislative scrutiny (PLS) is slowly starting to capture the attention of Parliaments with Westminster heritage around the world with its promise of improving the implementation and quality of law making through systematic review. Whether codified and structured, such as in the case of the United Kingdom (UK) Parliament, or ad hoc in nature, such as in the case of the Australian Parliament, review of the impact or implementation of enacted legislation is an integral part of the modern legislative process. Describing what is meant by PLS is challenging if the goal is to articulate the concept with universal application and appeal, but evaluating its place in the legislative process is critical for all modern democracies. The need to review, test and evaluate the effectiveness of existing laws is particularly pronounced in the context of growing distrust among the public when it comes to political institutions and traditional forms of democratic representation. PLS offers not just a way of checking that enacted laws have been implemented in practice, but also an opportunity to review whether the policy objectives underpinning those laws remain valid and supported by the community and a chance to consider as any intended consequences or unforeseen negative impacts. In this context, sharing insights and frameworks for evaluating scrutiny systems is inherently valuable, not just for jurisdictions like Australia, with a federal structure that provides multiple points of comparison and distinction, but also for the many diverse democracies that have Westminster heritage.

This Article aims to provide a new perspective from which to evaluate existing and proposed models of PLS by reflecting on the Australia ad hoc system of legislative scrutiny that occurs at the federal level. Using two case studies: one concerning the decade-long debate over the definition of 'marriage' in the *Marriage Act 1961* (Cth) and the other relating to a review of the *Sex Discrimination Act 1984* (Cth), this article offers insights into how PLS might be used as a vehicle to re-engage citizens with the parliamentary law-making process. The case studies explored in this article highlight the need for structural and procedural reforms in Australia to improve the quality and consistent of legislative scrutiny, particularly of laws that impact significantly on individual rights. However, the case studies also demonstrate that the same features of the current Australian model that have led rights advocates to raise concerns about its capacity to deliver robust legislative change might have important benefits when it comes to engaging a broad spectrum of public and parliamentary engagement in scrutiny and review. In other words, while Australia has much to learn from jurisdictions like the UK when it comes to reviewing existing laws, other jurisdictions can learn from the legislative scrutiny experience Down Under.

What is post legislative scrutiny?

Post legislative scrutiny (PLS) refers to the practice of reviewing enacted laws to determine whether the provisions have been implemented or enforced, and to evaluate the impact or effectiveness of the laws (Law Commission of England and Wales, 2006). The term has become increasingly popular in academic commentary (Caygill, 2019; Clapinska 2006; De Vrieze, 2019; Kelly and Everett, 2013; Kuchava, 2019; Moulds, 2019a) and development discourse following the work of the Law Commission of England and Wales on the topic in 2006, and more recently through the international development activities led by the Westminster Foundation for Democracy (WFD) (De Vrieze and Hasson, 2018). In response to the 2006 Law Commission Report, a systematic approach to PLS has been developed in the UK Parliament, wherein government departments prepare and publish a report that contains an assessment of whether an Act has met its key objectives within three to five years of the Act coming into force (Caygill, 2019, p. 296; Office of Leader of House of Commons, 2008, pp. 8–9 and 15). In its response to the Law Commission's Report, the Government did not establish a new specialist House of Commons committee to undertake post-legislative scrutiny. Instead it sought to integrate this role into the existing Select Committees system, supported by guidance material for government departments who are required to prepare a 'Memorandum' on appropriate Acts which are then considered by the relevant Commons departmental select committee (Kelly and Everett, 2013, pp. 5–6; Office of Leader of House of Commons, 2008). According to the Cabinet Office's Guide to Making Legislation (2013, updated 2017), these Memorandums should be prepared within three to five years after the Act in question has received Royal Assent and is intended to provide a preliminary assessment of how the law is working in practice, having regard to any objectives or benchmarks identified when the law was first considered by the Parliament (Cabinet Office, 2017, p. 294). The Memorandum is published as a 'Command Paper' and the relevant House Select Committee then decides whether it wishes to conduct a more detailed review of the (Act Guide to Making Legislation, 2017, pp. 294–300). Kelly and Everett have explained that in some instances this can lead to a different parliamentary body, such as a House of Lords Committee or Joint Committee conducting further scrutiny of the enacted legislation (2013, p. 6). The objective is to ensure that all Acts receive some degree of PLS, with a smaller handful of legislation being considered on in a more detailed way. While there remain concerns that this system is not reaching its full potential due to lack of adequate resourcing (House of Lords, Leader's Group on Working Practice, 2011, paras 139–141; Kelly and Everett, 2013, p. 13) this system has now generated a number of PLS reports that have themselves been subject to evaluation for effectiveness and impact (Kelly and Everett, 2013, pp. 91–6; Russell and Gover, 2017).

The UK systematic approach to PLS has also influenced the development of similar practices in other jurisdictions, particularly those with Westminster heritage, or those jurisdictions in receipt of development assistance from UK donors or aid agencies, including the WFD (see e.g. De Vrieze and Hasson, 2018). Similarly systematic approaches to PLS also exist within a range of diverse parliamentary settings, including in Indonesia (Wijananto, 2018, pp. 22–26), Lebanon (Mouawad, 2018, pp. 29–31) and Montenegro (Sosic, 2018, pp. 26–29) where specialist parliamentary committees exist to conduct PLS on a systematic basis. Some of these approaches were recently discussed in detail at a Asian Seminar on Post Legislative Scrutiny hosted by the Westminster Foundation of Democracy in 2019 in Yangon, Myanmar (see e.g. De Vrieze, 2019, pp. i–iii). As Parliaments in the Asian look to address historical challenges associated with governmental accountability and policy implementation, the demand for systematic approaches to PLS has grown, with a number of newly emerging parliamentary democracies seeking to learn from the UK experience (see e.g. Htun, 2019; Jeyabalan and Nordin, 2019).

Despite these developments, the term remains largely unknown among lawyers and political scientists outside of the UK, including in Australia. This is not because PLS is absent in these or other jurisdictions, or because it is not valued, but rather because the process of post-enactment review of laws is described differently in different jurisdictions, and often undertaken on an ad hoc basis. As observed in the *Statute Law Review* '[e]valuating the impact and effect of legislation once it has been enacted is a well-recognised and important element of the cyclical nature of most legislative endeavour' (Editorial, Statute Law Review, 2006, p. iii), but in many jurisdictions it is not approached in a systematic way. The scope of PLS also varies across jurisdictions, and across disciplines. A lawyer may take the view that PLS should focus on the constitutionality or lawfulness of the enacted law, an economist may demand a cost–benefit analysis of the law's implementation and a sociologist may seek to evaluate its impact on the community. This gives PLS an elusive character, despite the broad acceptance of its extrinsic value.

For example, in Australia PLS is a not a commonly used term, and if asked, most lawyers and political scientist would say that PLS occurs in a range of different forms within the Australian system (all of which can be described as ad hoc in nature and outcome). Sometimes, this takes the form of court-led PLS, such as judicial review of legislation to determine whether it is constitutional or not (see e.g. Stubbs, 2012), a process clearly different in nature to what the Law Commission of England and Wales had in mind. A second form of PLS in the Australian system is review that occurs in by parliamentary committees in response to a sunset provision or as part of a thematic reference made to the relevant committee by one House of Parliament. This form of PLS aligns more closely with the way the term has developed in the UK, although as will be discussed below, in the Australian context, there is no systematic framework for this type of PLS to take place (see e.g. Grenfell and Moulds, 2018; Rishi et al., 2012). A final form of PLS in Australia arises from the ad hoc review of enacted legislation by extra-parliamentary bodies including statutory authorities or Commissions (Williams and Burton, 2015).

These different forms of PLS underscore the dynamic nature of the concept of legislative scrutiny – and its close relationship with the constitutional culture of the particular jurisdiction in which it is being carried out (Stephenson 2016). In jurisdictions such as Australia, where there is a general scepticism of the need for codified or mandated approaches to legislative scrutiny (outside of a few discrete areas such as counter-terrorism laws) (Moulds 2016, 2018), it is not surprising that an ad hoc approach to PLS has developed. In the Australian context, it is also not surprising that there appears to be a blurry line between pre-enactment and post-enactment legislative scrutiny.

As the two case studies set out below demonstrate, at the federal level in Australia it is often hard to distinguish between an organically-driven process of law reform (such as a community push for 'marriage equality') and what might be described as an ad hoc form of PLS (such as a periodic review of the practical implementation of the provisions of the *Marriage Act*). This makes the Australian experience different to that in other Westminster Parliaments that have more systematic approaches to both pre-enactment and post-enactment legislative scrutiny, and more clearly prescribed scrutiny criteria (such as human rights legislation or prescribed legislative standards). While this distinction has led some in Australia to advocate for significant changes to be made to the way laws are scrutinised before and after enactment (see e.g. Debeljak & Grenfell, 2019; Fletcher, 2018) in this Article I suggest that despite its vulnerabilities the Australian ad hoc experience has something to offer scholars of PLS, particularly from the perspective of creating a deliberative environment for PLS to occur.

While the need for broad community participation in PLS has been recognised by actors such as the WFD (see e.g. De Vrieze 2018, Principle 13), executive control over which laws should be reviewed and what criteria should be applied remains a common feature of many jurisdictions that have adopted a systematic approach to post-enactment review. For example, pursuant to the UK Cabinet Office's Guide to Making Legislation, the criteria for PLS should largely be determined by the executive government at the pre-introduction stage, through the articulation of an impact assessment that accompanies the Bill's passage through Parliament (Cabinet Office, 2017, p. 129). This impact assessment then forms the standard against which the implementation of the enacted law is assessed. While this type of executive-led, systematic approach can deliver important transparency benefits and sometimes even legislative or policy change (Caygill, 2019, pp. 302–310), as discussed below, it has implications for the extent to which the community or other non-parliamentary can influence the scope of PLS, or actively participate in the PLS process.

Of course, the alternatives to executive controlled PLS can be equally problematic, and typically fall into two categories: a complete absence of meaningful review of enacted laws (such as complete lack of response by the Government of the day to any community-led attempts at review) or ad hoc post-legislative scrutiny undertaken by a variety of state and non-state actors, with varying rates of success. For this reason, jurisdictions without systematic or prescribed PLS processes, such as Australia, have generally been dismissed when it comes to compiling lessons for emerging parliamentary democracies seeking to improve the quality of post-enactment review. This article challenges this view. It suggests that those jurisdictions with ad hoc forms of PLS, such as Australia, continue to hold lessons for other jurisdictions. In particular, they can be used to highlight the benefits of integrating the role of the people or the community in both the conceptual understanding of what PLS *is*, and in the *way* that PLS is conducted.

Why engage in PLS?

According to the Law Commission of England and Wales, PLS can help ensure that enacted laws are being implemented in practice, are giving effect to the 'policy aims avowed' and not having any unintended consequences (Law Commission of England and Wales, 2005). Structured forms of PLS can also provide a 'new and significant role for Parliament' by closing the 'scrutiny loop' that begins with pre-enactment scrutiny (usually by specific parliamentary committees) and ends with PLS (Calpinska, 2006, p. 192; Norton, 2005). The broader aims or benefits of PLS have been articulated by aid organisations such as the WFD in its *London Declaration on Post Legislative Scrutiny* (2018), which provides that PLS works as a safeguard against the misuse of power by governments and as a way to monitor whether laws are benefiting citizens as originally intended. Other benefits of PLS derived from the Declaration include its potential to 'increase legislators' focus on implementation and delivery of policy aims and to improve government accountability. The Declaration also points to broader, normative aims that are rights enhancing in nature. For example, principle 4 of the Declaration provides that:

> Post Legislative Scrutiny provides an opportunity to assess the impact of legislation on the well-being of citizens and to address any unforeseen disadvantages or inequalities that may have been created based on gender, education, geographic location, disability, sexuality, income, religious ethnicity, language or other factors. A focus on inclusion supports greater monitoring and oversight of policy commitments to gender equality and human rights, and it furthers the SDG guiding principles of leaving no one behind. (Principle 4)

In other words, the key beneficiary of PLS is the citizen, or the public at large, with important flow on benefits for public confidence in democratic institutions – a chance to (re)build a positive relationship between the governors and the governed. This is a laudable goal, but one that this article argues can only be achieved if the PLS provides meaningful opportunities for meaningful public engagement at both the 'trigger' and 'process' stages, through a *deliberative approach* to scrutinising enacted legislation (Elster 1998; Gutmann and Thompson, 1996; Orr and Levy, 2016). The key features of a deliberative approach to making and reviewing laws is set out below.

Deliberative law making

The process of deliberation denotes a weighing up of different pieces of evidence or considering a range of different arguments or reasons before arriving at a decision. Deliberative decision-making also assumes that those members of the community who will be subject to collective decision should have the chance to have a say in the process (Elster 1998; Gutmann and Thompson, 1996; Orr and Levy, 2016) and the final decision about what the law or policy should be should be determined by an exchange of reasons and the development of rational persuasion and argument (Habermas, 1995, p. 124).

As Levy and Orr explain, ideally deliberative law making should be inclusive, and open-minded, where key participants speak and well as listen and seek to extend beyond the notion of majoritarian rule, and given life to other shared, democratic values (Levy and Orr, 2016, pp. 76–80). Deliberative law making should go beyond the idea of favouring the interests of one group against another, and instead engage in an active search for what is common ground among different groups (Levy and Orr, 2016, pp. 76–80). This in turn sees decision-makers engaging in reflection and sometimes, changing their mind (Levy and Orr, 2016, pp. 1997–2000). This approach has similarities with legal empowerment and social justice theories, which suggest that a more *engaged* electorate, with greater access to the law making *process*, could improve the legitimacy of parliamentary law making and thus enhance the levels of trust associated with key political and law making institutions (see e.g. Liebenberg, 2018, p. 633).

As the case studies below illustrate, deliberative law making can take many forms, and can be facilitated by both conventional democratic forums (such as parliamentary committees undertaking public inquiries or government-led consultations on draft policies) and less conventional ways of engaging with the community (such as through hosting citizen juries, polling the electorate or undertaking surveys using social media).

This article argues that the Australian ad hoc approach to PLS can provide useful examples of the benefits and challenges associated with adopting convention and less conventional forms of community engagement in legislative scrutiny, that may provide useful insights for those jurisdictions seeking to implement systematic or prescribed forms of PLS.

Part 2: post-legislative scrutiny in Australia

Unsurprisingly, many features of the Australian approach to legislative scrutiny mirror those of United Kingdom – both Parliaments adopting Westminster traditions and conventions, including the process of establishing parliamentary committees to review proposed and existing legislation and report back to each House of Parliament. However, the Australian Parliament also has a range of different characteristics to its UK counterpart. For example, unlike many other modern parliamentary democracies, Australia does not have a constitutional or statutory Bill of Rights at the federal level, or a prescribed, systematic approach to legislative scrutiny. Instead, Australia relies on an 'exclusively parliamentary' model of rights protection (Williams and Burton, 2015) that revolves primarily around a Parliamentary Joint Committee on Human Rights and a requirement for new legislation to be introduced with statement of human rights compatibility (*Human Rights (Parliamentary Scrutiny) Act* 2011 (Cth)). In addition, unlike the UK, Australia is a federation of States and Territories, each with their own Parliaments and Governments, and with law making power delineated among these Parliaments via a written Constitution. At the federal level, the Australia Parliament comprises of two Houses – the House of Representatives (with members elected by constituents from equally sized electorates) and the Senate (with members elected on a proportional basis, to provide equal representation for each Australian State, and members from the two Territories) (see further Appleby, Grenfell and Reilly, 2019, pp. 130–143). The proportional composition of the Senate means that the Government of the day is less likely to hold the majority of Senate seats, and instead is required to win the support of independents, minor parties or the Opposition if it seeks to secure the passage of its Bills through both Houses of Parliament. The Senate is also home to many of the most powerful parliamentary committees, and for this reason, is often described as a *House of Review* (Mulgan, 1996). Through its standing and select committees it plays a central role in scrutinising proposed laws and executive action (Grenfell, 2015). The Senate Standing Orders provide some of these committees with broad powers to conduct public inquiries into Bills and other matters (described as 'inquiry-based committees'). These committees, such as the Senate Standing Committee on Legal and Constitutional Affairs, can also include 'participating members', (other members of parliament who join the committee for a particular inquiry), making them politically diverse and dynamic forums for engaging with contested policy issues.

The Senate Standing Orders also establish specific committees to scrutinise proposed laws with reference to certain prescribed criteria (described as 'scrutiny-committees'). The scrutiny-based committees include the Senate Standing Committee for the Scrutiny of Bills (Scrutiny of Bills Committee) and the Parliamentary Joint Committee on Human Rights (the Human Rights Committee). These scrutiny-based committees are required to review every single Bill (and in the case of the Human Rights Committee, all legislative instruments) for compliance with a range of scrutiny criteria, including criteria that relates to individual rights and liberties. These committees rarely hold public inquiries, but they regularly produce written reports and engage in correspondence with proponents of the Bill, highlighting any areas of concern or non-compliance with the scrutiny criteria. These scrutiny reports can then be used by the inquiry-based committees, or submission-makers to the inquiry-based committees, to draw attention to particularly concerning features of the proposed law or policy.

It is important to note that while some of these committees are required to scrutinise Bills, there is no corresponding duty to engage in scrutiny of enacted provisions, unless an existing law is specifically referred to a Committee for review. The Scrutiny of Bills Committee is given no powers to initiate inquiries into enacted legislation, and while the Human Rights Committee can review existing legislation for compliance with prescribed human rights, in practice it has exercised this power only very rarely. This means that there is no *systematic* approach to post legislative scrutiny in Australia. In addition, the Australian Parliaments does not employ the practice of memorandums of implementation like the British Parliament or mandate post-enactment scrutiny as part of a committee's primary role, like the Indonesian *Badan Legislasi* (De Vrieze and Hasson, 2018, pp. 14–17 and 24–26).

Trigger-points for PLS in Australia

In the Australian context there are four main triggers for post-enactment scrutiny of legislation: the inclusion of a sunset clause in the original legislation; the inclusion of a review provision in the original legislation; a specific referral by parliament to an external review body empowered to undertake post legislative scrutiny; and community-initiated parliamentary review. As the case studies below highlight, each of these triggers has the potential to involve deliberative practices, but some are more tightly controlled by the executive and the parliament than others.

Sunset clauses

'Sunset clause' is the name given to a legal provision which provides for the expiry of a law at a future point in time, providing a clear incentive for the Parliament to either review and re-enact the relevant provision, or allow it to be deleted from the statute books These types of provisions come in many different forms: they can list a date when the whole Act ceases to have legal effect (akin to automatic repeal); they can specify a date on which the legislation will lapse unless proactively reviewed and renewed by the Parliament (akin to a prompt for legislative affirmation) (Rishi et al., 2012, p. 307). In Australia, the latter approach to sunset clauses is most common, particularly with respect to legislation that is considered 'extraordinary' in nature, or enacted in response to an emergency situation (such as counter-terrorism measures or quarantine measures to protect public health), or containing features that abrogate or unduly infringe on individual rights (Finn 2010; Ip, 2013). The type of PLS triggered by sunset clauses is clearly tightly controlled by the Parliament, and the inclusion of such provisions in Australian legislation is often the result of a negotiation between the executive government and the 'cross bench' members of the Senate.

Review clauses

The use of review clauses in legislation is also a form of parliamentary-controlled, executive dominated PLS and is an increasingly common practice in Australian legislation that engages individual rights, such as counter-terrorism law-making (see e.g. Parliamentary Joint Committee on Intelligence and Security, 2018, para [1.10]). These clauses mandate review of the entire Act or parts of the Act within a certain time period, by a particular review body such as parliamentary committee or less commonly, a statutory agency or commission. For example, each major tranche of counter-terrorism legislation has been subject to mandatory and regular parliamentary review, for example through the use of specific review clauses (e.g. ASIO Amendment (Terrorism) Bill 2003 (Cth)) or referral to the specialist Intelligence and Security Committee or to external statutory review bodies such as the Independent National Security Legislation Monitor (e.g. Brandis and Turnbull, 2015). This type of 'dual scrutiny' approach to PLS also offers unique opportunities for deliberative decision making to take place as multiple decision makers (with slightly different incentives and different relationships with the Executive Government) engage with the community during the review process (Dalla-Pozza, 2019, pp. 673–700).

Referral to external review body

In addition to parliamentary committees, some bodies outside of the Australian Parliament have been granted a mandate or power to review enacted legislation against certain prescribed criteria, giving rise to an ad hoc system of extra-parliamentary post-legislative scrutiny at the federal level in Australia. Often these extra-parliamentary bodies have a statutory framework, with prescribed mandates, functions and powers that focus on a particular subject area or component of the Executive Government. For example, the Independent National Security Legislation Monitor (INSLM) is a statutory office established to review and report on the operation, effectiveness and implications of Australia's national security legislation (*Independent Monitor of National Security Legislation Act* 2010 (Cth) Part II). Other statutory bodies have review mandates that encompass a wide range of thematic areas of law making and are designed to 'sound the alarm' about laws that are not being implemented correctly, have unintended consequences, or unduly infringe on individual rights. For example, the Australian Human Rights Commission (AHRC), has an explicit statutory mandate to provide advice about the human rights compliance of Australia's federal laws (*Australian Human Rights Commission Act* 1986 (Cth) s11). This power is often exercised in the form of a public inquiry into a gap in the law which culminates in a written report containing recommendations for legislative and policy change (AHRC, 2007). The Australian Law Reform Commission (ALRC) also has statutory power to make recommendations for reform on topics selected by the Attorney-General. Over time the ALRC has proven to be a highly 'influential agent for legal reform in Australia', with over 85 per cent its recommendations either substantially or partially implemented by successive Australian governments (AHRC, 2019; French, 2015).

This form of PLS – which is also common across many modern parliamentary democracies – is less tightly controlled by the Parliament or the Executive Government, and has the potential to facilitate both conventional and non-conventional forms of deliberative law making, provided the statutory bodies concerned are appropriately resourced. However, as the work of the AHRC and the ALRC demonstrates, while both bodies can have powerful legislative impacts, in practice the legislative scrutiny they conduct is confined to only a very small handful of federal laws and is conducted on a thematic rather than systematic basis. This highlights the common trade-off between ad hoc and systematic approaches to PLS: the former may have a greater degree of independence and flexibility when it comes to deliberative engagement, but the latter has the potential to provides a more regular, consistent approach to reviewing enacted legislation.

Community-initiated parliamentary review of enacted legislation

In addition to the above 'top down' triggers for PLS in Australia, there is also the potential for PLS to occur in response to calls for review by the community (rather than as a result of a review process prescribed either by legislation or by government practice). For the purpose of this article, this is the form of PLS that is of most interest. This is because community-initiated PLS has the potential to be highly deliberative in nature, and provides fertile ground for experimenting with less conventional forms of parliamentary-community engagement. This is because community initiated PLS engages with a wide range of views and evidence not just when undertaking the review, but also when determining the scope and purpose of the review in the first place.

It can be hard to identify community led PLS, because public calls for legislative change are rarely framed in terms of scrutiny and review. More commonly, there is public campaign for the Government to change its policy in response to a certain issue – which is perhaps best understood as part of the 'regular' democratic process, rather than any form of 'legislative review'. But sometimes, the community is able to articulate with more precision the particular existing law that it wants to see reviewed, and the particular criteria it wants to see applied. In this article, I suggest that this what occurred with respect to the Senate Standing Committee on Legal and Constitutional Affairs' 2008 review into the effectiveness of the *Sex Discrimination Act 1984* (Cth) and with respect to the decade-long review of the provisions of the *Marriage Act 1961* (Cth), both of which are described below.

Case study 1: 2008 review of the sex discrimination act

In 2008, the Senate Standing Committee on Legal and Constitutional Affairs (the LCA Committee) conducted a review of the *Sex Discrimination Act 1984* (Cth) (SDA) which contained Australia's laws prohibiting discrimination against people on the grounds of sex and gender in prescribed areas of public life. It was the first review of the legislation in 10 years (Allen, 2009, pp. 100–108; LCA Committee, 2008, para [2.11]). It proved to be extensive both in terms of scope and public engagement.

The review was triggered by a range of factors, including the election of the Rudd Labor Government in 2007 (following more than a decade of the Howard Liberal Government being in power), and the highly diverse composition of the Senate. However, the Senate's decision to refer the SDA to the LCA Committee for inquiry and review was undoubtedly influenced by the work of community groups and advocates had been raising with parliamentarians for some time, as well as findings of past inquiries into aspects of the legislation (see e.g. House of Representatives Standing Committee on Legal and Constitutional Affairs, 1992). This is reflected in the terms of reference for the inquiry, which included questions such as the extent to which the legislation had been subject to judicial interpretations, its effectiveness at preventing intersecting forms of discrimination the scope of the existing exemptions in the law, whether the legislation was providing effective remedies and the impact of the legislation on state and territory laws (LCA Committee, 2008).

The conduct of the review also contained elements that align with the features of deliberative law-making described above. For example, the LCA Committee advertised the inquiry in *The Australian* newspaper and on the committee's website. The LCA Committee also wrote to over 140 organisations and individuals inviting written submissions. In response to these efforts, the LCA Committee received 81 written submissions and held public hearings in Sydney, Melbourne and Canberra, hearing from 39 different witnesses from a range of community organisations including the Law Council of Australia, Human Rights Law Resource Centre, Australian Education Union, UNIFEM Australia, Australian Council of Trade Unions, Carers ACT, Women's Electoral Lobby and Australian Christian Lobby (LCA Committee, 2008, paras [1.4]-[1.5]).

The LCA Committee made a suite of detailed recommendations following the inquiry, some of which called for legislative amendments, but others to changes in the way the laws were administered and understood by the community and those responsible for complying with the requirements set out in the law (Recommendation 34). The LCA Committee also staggered the implementation of its recommendations, suggesting some changes that could be introduced immediately, changes for further consideration over the next 12 months and longer-term changes which require additional consultation (Chapter 11).

Some of the most significant, and controversial, recommendations responded to community calls to clarify or reconceptualise key aspects of the legislation's policy aims and scope. For example, the LCA Committee recommended that the legislation be amended to better accommodate family and carer responsibilities and to expand the powers of the Australian Human Rights Commission to address systemic discrimination (Recommendations 14 and 29). It also recommended amending complaint handling procedures, increasing funding provided to working women's centres, community legal centres, providing low cost legal services and legal aid to ensure that they have the resources to provide advice about sex discrimination and sexual harassment matters; and extending the reach of individual complaints by enabling courts to order corrective and preventative remedies (Recommendations 19 and 23).

The nature of these recommendations differs significantly from the type of recommendations more commonly arising from PLS that is mandated by legislation (for example by sunset provisions) or executive controlled (for example by the issue of departmental reports). The strong community response to the inquiry, and the genuine efforts of deliberation adopted by the committee, led to a reconceptualization the policy aims of the legislation or altering the resourcing provided to government and non-government agencies involved in the implementation of legislative provisions. Unsurprisingly, not all of these resource-intensive recommendations have been fully implemented by Government following the inquiry. This fact highlights one of the other common trade-offs between ad hoc forms of PLS and those more tightly controlled by the executive government: the more distance the body engaging in the review has from the executive government, the less like its recommendations for change will be implemented.

However, if a longer term view of the value of the 2008 SDA review is taken, it is possible to discern a significant, positive impact both in terms of Australia's laws and policies relating to sex discrimination, and on the way law makers engage with the community. For example, in 2013 amendments to the SDA were introduced to by the federal Government that responded to many of the LCA Committee's recommendations and sparked similar inquiries and legislative amendments across a number of Australian States (*Sex Discrimination Amendment (Sexual Orientation, Gender Identity and Intersex Status) Act* 2013 (Cth)). In addition, the detailed report prepared by the LCA Committee has proven to be of central importance in subsequent advocacy by community groups calling for improvements to Australia's anti-discrimination regime. For example, it became an important foundation for the Sex Discrimination Commissioner to commence separate inquiries into the Treatment of Women in the Australian Defence Force (during 2011–2013) (AHRC, 2013) and for the AHRC to publish the 2010 Gender Equality Blueprint acknowledging the impact of violence against women on the lives of

Australians and setting out a range of strategies and recommendations for improved responses. The LCA Committee's inquiry into the SDA was also a catalyst for the 2009 Productivity Commission's inquiry into Paid Maternity, Paternity and Parental Leave (Australian Productivity Commission, 2009), which in turn led to the adoption of Australia's first paid parental leave scheme in 2011. Undoubtedly, politics played a key role in each of these developments, however at the very least, this case study demonstrates the flow-on implications of encouraging community input into the scope of review being undertaken, as well as the review itself. It also highlights some of the challenges and benefits of adopting deliberative forms of PLS in conjunction with more conventional forms of parliamentary committee based legislative review.

Case study 2: multi-committee scrutiny of the marriage act 1961 (Cth)

Another example of supplementing conventional forms of legislative review with less conventional deliberative techniques can be found in the numerous parliamentary committee reviews of the *Marriage Act 1961* (Cth) during the decade long 'marriage equality' debate in Australia. Some may describe these reviews as falling within the 'pre-legislative scrutiny' category as they were connected to private member's attempts to introduce amendments to the *Marriage Act*. However, it is also possible to describe the multiple committee hearings as a collective form of PLS, evaluating whether the provisions of the *Marriage Act* have been implemented or enforced, and to evaluate the impact or effectiveness of the law. Even if this characterisation is rejected, and the parliamentary inquiries into the *Marriage Act* are considered outside of the scope of PLS, the way the committees experimented with deliberative law making techniques should remain of interest to those contemplating ways to improve the quality of legislative review at either the pre or post enactment stage.

The LCA Committee's 2009 inquiry into the Marriage Equality Amendment Bill 2009 (Cth) (the 2009 Bill) is one particularly significant example of the deliberative role the parliamentary committee system can play, even when legislative change is not immediately forthcoming. The 2009 Bill, introduced by Australian Greens Senator Sarah Hanson-Young, aimed to reverse the effect of the 2004 amendments to ensure that all couples, regardless of gender, could access legal marriage and have their overseas marriages recognised in Australia. The Bill was referred to the Government-majority LCA Legislation Committee for inquiry and report, and generated a then-record number of submissions, in excess of 28,000 – so many that it was not physically possible for the Committee to publish them all (LCA Committee, 2009, Appendix 1). Of these submissions, approximately 11,000 were in favour of the Bill, and approximately 17,000 were opposed (LCA Committee

2009, Appendix 1). The submissions received by the Committee, coupled with the public hearing held in Melbourne, focused on the issues such as the relationship between the institution of marriage and internationally protected human rights (LCA Committee, 2009 at paras [2.21]–[2.25]); the impact of non-heterosexual marriage on children (at paras [2.29]–[2.32]); the dynamic nature of marriage as an institution and the growing diversity of Australian families (at paras [3.6]–[3.14]); and relevant reforms in other comparable jurisdictions that permitted equal access to legal marriage regardless of gender or sexual orientation. These included reforms in Belgium (2003), Spain (2005), Canada (2005), South Africa (2006), Norway (2007) and Sweden (2009), (see LCA Committee, 2009, at paras[2.18]–[2.20] and [2.26]–[2.28]).

These issues were explored in detail in the LCA Legislation Committee's report, displaying many of the features of reflective, inclusive, broad-sourced decision-making described by scholars as important to deliberative law-making (Levy and Orr, 2016; Uhr, 1998, pp. 10–11): features that were largely absent from the broader political and media debate at that time. The next year, Senator Hanson-Young introduced a similar Bill (the 2010 Bill), which was again referred to the LCA Legislation Committee for inquiry and report (LCA Committee, 2012). Another record was reached when the Committee received approximately 79,200 submissions: approximately 46,400 submissions in support of the 2010 Bill, and approximately 32,800 submissions opposed (LCA Committee 2012, para [1.32]). The sheer volume of submissions received made this inquiry a powerful indicator of a shift in public support in favour of marriage equality and the issues discussed in the LCA Committee's report proved to be predictive of the political conflicts that would dominate much of the public debate on reform in this area for more than a decade.

These parliamentary-based forms of PLS of the *Marriage Act* in Australia were subsequently supplemented by efforts to more directly engage the Australian community in the form of a voluntary 'postal survey' of all Australians on the electoral roll as to their views on 'whether or not the law should be changed to allow same-sex couples to marry.(McKeown, 2018). Nearly eighty per cent of Australians had answered the survey and the majority indicated that the law should be changed to allow same-sex couples to marry, with 61.6 per cent responding 'Yes' 38.4 per cent responding 'No' (Australian Bureau of Statistics, 2017). On the same day, Liberal Senator Dean Smith introduced the Marriage Amendment (Definition and Religious Freedoms) Bill 2017 with features similar to those explored by the LCA Committee described above. This Bill was enacted into law in 2018.

Even taken together, it is hard to claim that the legislative review work of these parliamentary committees delivered 'marriage equality' reform for Australia. Clearly party politics played an important role in securing parliamentary support for the Dean Smith Bill. However, the deliberative law making facilitated by these committees – and supplemented by the less conventional forms of community engagement such as the 'postal survey' approach – could be described as the catalyst for key individuals to 'change their mind' and ultimately support the reforms introduced in 2017 (see further Moulds, 2019, pp. 745–786). This is because these parliamentary committees created a safe space for a range of key participants to share lived experiences, exchange expert evidence, reflect on comparative jurisdictions, and negotiate solutions to genuine concerns (Moulds, 2019, pp. 745–786). This article argues that by facilitating such a high degree of community engagement, across a wide range of platforms, this ad hoc approach to legislative view was able to achieve significant legal and social change, in a way that a more tightly prescribed process (reliant for example on either sunset clauses or departmental reporting) may have struggled to achieve.

As discussed below, these two case studies are not intended to refute the need for prescribed, systematic forms of PLS to be adopted in modern parliamentary democracies. Rather they are included to encourage those interested in improving the quality of parliamentary law making to consider how to integrate deliberative law making opportunities or techniques into legislative review, and to reflect on both the costs and benefits associated with executive-controlled forms of PLS.

Part 3: towards a more deliberative approach to PLS

As discussed above, the conventional approach to legislative review in Westminster Parliaments has been heavily influenced by the principles of representative decision-making and responsible government, giving rise to a number of assumptions of about the agency of key actors within the system. In line with this approach, it is the elected representatives in the Parliament, often controlled or dominated by the Executive Government, that determine when PLS occurs, how it occurs, the scrutiny criteria that applies and sets the practical and political limits on what the outcomes of PLS might be. When implemented in some jurisdictions, this has taken the form of a specialist PLS committee or departmental reporting process, with prescribed time frames, and pre-determined scrutiny criteria.

The Australian approach to legislative scrutiny at the federal level is far less structured or prescribed, and as a result has been criticised for lacking rigour and being susceptible to executive dominance. However, despite these perceived shortcomings, investigations into the impact of parliamentary scrutiny in Australia have found that that parliamentary committees and other statutory-based scrutiny bodies have had a significant impact on the content and implementation of federal laws (Grenfell and Moulds 2018; Moulds 2016, 2018). Moreover, the Australian experience suggests that there are distinct benefits in retaining a level of flexibility and diversity when it comes to which bodies are charged with undertaking legislative review, and what review criteria should apply. The Australian experience suggests that different review bodies are able to forge different relationships with key actors: some forming trusted connections with key executive agencies enabling a safe space for policy alternatives to be explored; others experimenting with new ways of engaging directly with the public on the effectiveness of enacted laws, or responding to community-led calls for review of enacted laws.

For example, the Scrutiny of Bills Committee has a long-serving membership, a practice of issuing unanimous reports, a well-entrenched scrutiny mandate that is accepted across the political spectrum, giving it authority to produce 'technical scrutiny' reports on existing and proposed laws. These reports rarely provide recommendations for specific legislative change, but on the other hand, often form the basis of 'best practice' guidance for legislative drafters and policy makers involved in formulating new laws or amendments to existing laws (Department of Prime Minister and Cabinet, 2017, para [5.52]). Working in isolation, such a Committee might offer little when it comes to effective PLS, but when placed within a broader scrutiny system, its reports help provide an authoritative analysis of the law that can facilitate reflection and review by other actors in other forums.

Other committees within the Australian system have particularly strong deliberative aspects, such as the LCA Committees, whose legitimacy is sometimes questioned by the government of the day, but whose relatively broad and diverse range of participants give it particular strengths when it comes to community engagement and influencing public debate on proposed or existing laws. As noted in the case study examples described above, these inquiry-based Senate Standing Committees regularly hold public inquiries into the impact and effectiveness of existing laws and are open to experimenting with new forms of direct community engaging, such as the use of online 'survey monkey' surveys (Baker 2018; LCA Committee, Citizenship Bill Report, 2018) online questionnaires (House Standing Committee on Social Policy and Legal Affairs, 2015) and other social media forums (Baczynski, 2009; Duffy and Foley, 2011; House Standing Committee on Health and Aging, 2007).

If relied upon exclusively as triggers or conduits of PLS such techniques would clearly give rise to concerns, including concerns relating to majoritarian decision making. This can be seen in the marriage equality example, where the use of direct democracy mechanisms, such as plebiscites or postal surveys, brought strong criticism from those concerned by the prospect of allowing for majoritarian views to determine the legal protection of rights held by vulnerable minority groups (ABC Radio National, 2016; Pettit, 2001). However, when combined with other components within the Australian scrutiny system, in particularly when used in the context of broader parliamentary committee scrutiny, these techniques can help to rebuild relationships between parliamentarians and their electorates, and provide new ways to directly engage the public with the law making process.

These qualities appear to be recognised by the UK Government in its response to the Law Reform Commission's 2006 report on PLS, which sought to invest existing committees within the UK Parliament with PLS functions (as an alternative to creating a new PLS Committee). However, by tying the process of PLS with the impact assessment that accompanied the relevant law at the time of its passage through Parliament, the UK approach to PLS is tightly controlled by the executive, and leaves little room for experimentation with deliberative approaches to determining both the scope and outcome of subsequent reviews of the law.

In contrast, the 2008 review of the Australian *Sex Discrimination Act* demonstrates the benefits of providing a direct avenue for citizens to themselves 'trigger' review of existing laws, and to directly contribute to both the scrutiny criteria to be applied and to the process of undertaking the review. Whilst the Australian system does not currently have a formalised system for citizen-initiated PLS, it does have a well-established petition process that could be combined with the existing parliamentary committee referral processes (see e.g. Senate Standing Order 24A) and used as a model for a more structured approach to citizen-led PLS in Australia.

These opportunities for experimentation within the Australian system arise precisely because it lacks mandated or structured approach to PLS. It does not seek to invest one particular parliamentary or external independent body with the task of reviewing enacted laws to consider whether they have been implemented effectively or whether they have had any unintended consequences. Whilst this may be seen as a weakness by some (see e.g. Williams and Burton, 2015; Williams and Reynolds, 2016), it allows the Australian system to generate a culture of rights scrutiny that permeates beyond party-political lines and extends to those working 'behind the scenes' on policy development and legislative drafting. Again, this Australian culture of rights scrutiny (developed without any constitutional or statutory backing, and instead reliant upon particular practice) may be considered weak or deficient in important respects, but the examples set out above and documented in related research (Moulds 2018) suggest that it can have sustainable rights-enhancing impacts and provide important opportunities to engage parliamentarians and law makers in deliberative processes. For these reasons, other jurisdictions looking to implement or improve PLS processes may benefit from considering how to loosen executive control over post enactment review, or at least distribute scrutiny functions across a range of parliamentary review bodies, with a focus on providing space for innovation and experimentation when it comes to community engagement.

Part 4: conclusion

As Russell and Benton observe in their work on legislative scrutiny in the UK, the complex and dynamic nature of parliamentary committees and other legislative scrutiny bodies means evaluating their performance is not always straightforward (see e.g. Kavanagh, 2015; Larkin, Hindmoor and Kenyon 2009; Russell & Benton, 2009; Tolley 2009). Seeking to draw broad lessons from a small number of case studies from a particular jurisdiction is should be approached with great care. This Article does not suggest that the above Australian experiences provide a template for effective PLS elsewhere. Indeed, this Article acknowledges and accepts the significant limitations of the Australian model of legislative review, particularly when it comes to achieving consistent, regular review that results in practical change (Debeljak & Grenfell 2019; Fletcher, 2018).

However, the examples outlined above demonstrate that there are positive aspects of the existing Australian model of legislative scrutiny, particularly when the ad hoc components of the Australian system are viewed as whole. As documented in related research (Grenfell and Moulds 2018; Moulds 2016, 2018), despite (or perhaps because of) its many disparate components, the Australian parliamentary scrutiny system can have a positive impact on the content of federal law, and can provide a meaningful deliberative forum for community engagement. For this reason, the Australian experience provides a different standpoint from which to consider the role and benefits of PLS, and to identify new opportunities for incorporating deliberative features into scrutiny models elsewhere. In particular, this Article suggests that scrutiny systems that incorporate a range of different attributes and actors may be particularly well placed to deliver on the stated aims and benefits of PLS, particularly when accompanied by other means of engaging directly with the public.

As discussed in Part II, the challenge for those seeking to design new models of PLS (for implementation in either emerging or established parliamentary democracies) is to successfully navigate the trade-offs that exist between ad hoc systems of review and executive-controlled systems of review. These include the tension between facilitating a truly deliberative review process and generating the required political support to effect change; and the tension between encouraging community-led PLS and providing consistent, transparent, government reporting on the implementation of enacted laws.

The Australian system is far from perfect when it comes to navigating these tensions or delivering on the broad aims of PLS as set out in the WDF's *London Declaration*. But it may provide some important insights into how existing parliamentary mechanisms can be adapted or built upon to facilitate a more deliberative approach to PLS, and encourage other jurisdictions who lack systematic approaches to legislative review to reflect on the positive aspects of their existing scrutiny systems.

Disclosure statement

No potential conflict of interest was reported by the author(s).

ORCID

Sarah Moulds http://orcid.org/0000-0003-3246-0987

References

ABC Radio National. (2016). The problem with plebiscites: The limits of democracy and the nature of representation. *Religion and Ethics*. 2 September 2016 (Waleed Aly). Retrieved January 4, 2020 from https://www.abc.net.au/religion/the-problem-with-plebiscites-the-limits-of-democracy-and-the-nat/10096592

Allen, D. (2009). Improving the effectiveness of the Sex discrimination act recommendations from the 2008 Senate inquiry. *Australian Journal of Labour Law, 22*(1), 100–108.

Appleby, G., Reilly, A., & Grenfell, L. (2019). *Australian public law* (3rd ed., pp. 169–171). Oxford: Oxford University Press.

ASIO Amendment (Terrorism) Bill 2003 (Cth).

Australian Bureau of Statistics (Cth). (2017). Australian marriage law postal survey, 2017 (Media Release, 1800.0, 15 November 2017). Retrieved January 4, 2020 from http://www.abs.gov.au/ausstats/abs@.nsf/mf/1800.0

Australian Human Rights Commission. (2007). *Same-sex: Same entitlements final report*. Retrieved February 7, 2020 from https://www.humanrights.gov.au/our-work/lgbti/publications/same-sex-same-entitlements

Australian Human Rights Commission. (2013). *Report into the treatment of women in the Australian defence force*. Retrieved February 7, 2020 from https://www.humanrights.gov.au/our-work/sex-discrimination/projects/review-treatment-women-australian-defence-force

Australian Human Rights Commission Act 1986 (Cth) s11.

Australian Human Rights Commission: About. (2019, May 25). *Australian human rights commission website*. https://www.humanrights.gov.au/about

Australian Productivity Commission. (2009). *Report into paid parental leave*. Retrieved February 7, 2019 from https://www.pc.gov.au/inquiries/completed/parental-support/report

Baczynski J. (2009). *Opportunities for greater consultation? House committees use of information and communication technologies*. Parliamentary studies paper 8, Crawford School of Economics & Government, ANU, Canberra, 2009, 1.

Baker, E. (2018, April 27). Parliament's use of survey monkey slammed by students, Hanson. *The Canberra Times*. https://www.canberratimes.com.au/story/6018443/parliaments-use-of-surveymonkey-slammed-by-students-hanson/

Brandis, G., & Turnbull, M. (2015, April 3). *Government response to committee report on the telecommunications (interception and access) amendment (data retention) bill 2014*. Media Release.

Calpinska, L. (2006). Post-legislative scrutiny of acts of parliament. *Commonwealth Law Bulletin*, 32(2), 191–204. https://doi.org/10.1080/03050710600907015

Caygill, T. (2019). Legislation under review: An assessment of post-legislative scrutiny recommendations in the UK parliament. *The Journal of Legislative Studies*, 25(2), 295–313. https://doi.org/10.1080/13572334.2019.1603260

Dalla-Pozza, D. (2019). Dual scrutiny mechanism for Australia's counter-terrorism law landscape: The INSLM and the PJCIS. In J. Debeljak & L. Grenfell (Eds.), *Law- making and human rights Sydney: Thompson Reuters* (pp. 673–700). Thompson Reuters.

De Vrieze, F. (2018) *Principles of post-legislative scrutiny by parliaments*. Westminster Foundation for Democracy. Retrieved January 10, 2020 from https://www.wfd.org/approach/post-legislative-scrutiny/

De Vrieze, F. (2019). Preface on post legislative scrutiny. *Journal of Southeast Asian Human Rights*, 3(2), i–iii. https://doi.org/10.19184/jseahr.v3i2.14747

De Vrieze, F., & Hasson, V. (2018). *Post legislative scrutiny: Comparative practices of post-legislative scrutiny in selected parliaments and the rationale for its place in democracy assistance*. Westminster Foundation for Democracy. Retrieved January 10, 2020 from https://www.wfd.org/wp-content/uploads/2018/07/Comparative-Study-PLS-WEB.pdf

Debeljak, J., & Grenfell, L. (Eds.). (2019). *Law- making and human rights*. Thompson Reuters.

Department of Prime Minister and Cabinet. (2017, February). Government of Australian. *Legislation Handbook*, 5, 52.

Duffy, B., & Foley, M. (2011). Social media, community engagement and perceptions of parliament: A case study from the NSW legislative council. *Australasian Parliamentary Review*, 198–206. https://www.parliament.nsw.gov.au/lc/articles/Documents/social-media-community-engagement-and-perception/17-DuffyandFoley-Social Media.pdf

Editorial. (2006). Post-legislative scrutiny. *Statute Law Review*, 27(2), iii–ivi. https://doi.org/10.1093/slr/hml001

Elster, J. (1998). Introduction. In J. Elster (Ed.), *Deliberative democracy* (pp. 1–18). Cambridge University Press.

Finn, J. E. (2010). Sunset clauses and democratic deliberation: Assessing the significance of sunset provisions in antiterrorism legislation. *Columbia Journal of Transnational Law*, 442–502.

Fletcher, A. (2018). *Australia's human rights scrutiny regime*. Melbourne University Press.
French, R. (2015, October 23). ALRC 40th anniversary celebration. Speech delivered at the Australian Law Reform Commission, Sydney. Online: Australian Law Reform Commission. Retrieved February 7, 2020 from https://www.alrc.gov.au/news-media/speech/alrc-40th-anniversary-celebration-french
Grenfell, L. (2015). An Australian spectrum of political rights scrutiny: Continuing to lead by example? *Public Law Review, 26*(1), 19–38.
Grenfell, L., & Moulds, S. (2018). The role of committees in rights protection in federal and state parliaments in Australia. *University of New South Wales Law Journal, 41*(1), 40–79. http://classic.austlii.edu.au/au/journals/UNSWLawJl/2018/3.html
Gulati Rishi, G., McGarrity, N., & Williams, G. (2012). Sunset clauses in Australian anti-terror laws. *Adelaide Law Review, 33*, 307–333. http://www.austlii.edu.au/au/journals/UNSWLRS/2013/14.html
Gutmann, A., & Thompson, D. F. (1996). *Democracy and disagreement*. Harvard University Press.
Habermas, J. (1995). Reconciliation through the public use of reason: Remarks on John Rawls's political liberalism. *The Journal of Philosophy, 92*(3), 109–131. https://doi.org/10.5840/jphil199592335
House of Lords, Leader's Group on Working Practices. (2011). *Report of the leader's group on working practices* (April 2011, HL 136) at paras 139–141. Retrieved February 7, 2020 from https://publications.parliament.uk/pa/ld201012/ldselect/ldspeak/136/136.pdf
House of Representatives Standing Committee on Legal and Constitutional Affairs. (1992). *Half way to equal: Report of the inquiry into equal opportunity and equal status for women in Australia*.
House Standing Committee on Health and Aging. (2007). Parliament of Australia. *Inquiry into Breastfeeding* (2007). Retrieved January 4, 2020 from https://www.aph.gov.au/Parliamentary_Business/Committees/House_of_Representatives_Committees?url=haa/breastfeeding/report.htm
House Standing Committee on Social Policy and Legal Affairs. (2015). Parliament of Australia. *From conflict to cooperation inquiry into the child support program*. Retrieved January 4, 2020 from https://www.aph.gov.au › Child Support Program › Report › fullreport
Htun, S. Y. (2019). Legal aspects of the right to nationality pursuant to Myanmar citizenship law. *Journal of Southeast Asian Human Rights, 3*(2), 277–299. https://doi.org/10.19184/jseahr.v3i2.13480
Human Rights (Parliamentary Scrutiny) Act 2011 (Cth).
Independent Monitor of National Security Legislation Act 2010 (Cth) Part II.
Ip, J. (2013). Sunset clauses and counterterrorism legislation. *Public Law, 74*.
Jeyabalan, R., & Nordin, R. (2019). Protection of the rights of the victims of human trafficking: Has Malaysia done enough? *Journal of Southeast Asian Human Rights, 3*(2), 300–316. https://doi.org/10.19184/jseahr.v3i2.9231
Kavanagh, A. (2015). The joint committee on human rights: A hybrid breed of constitutional watchdog. In M. Hunt, H. J. Hooper, & P. Yowell (Eds.), *Parliaments and human rights: Redressing the democratic deficit* (pp. 111–134). Hart Publishing.
Kelly, R., & Everett, M. (2013). Post-legislative scrutiny. House of Commons Library Standard Note. SN/PC/05232.

Kuchava, K. (2019). First post-legislative scrutiny in Georgia: Steps towards generating result-oriented laws. *Journal of Southeast Asian Human Rights*, 258–276. https://doi.org/10.19184/jseahr.v3i2.13600

Larkin, P., Hindmoor, A., & Kennon, A. (2009). Assessing the influence of select committees in the UK: The education and skills committee 1997–2005. *The Journal of Legislative Studies*, 15(1), 71–89. https://doi.org/10.1080/13572330802666844

Law Commission of England and Wales. (2005). Ninth Programme of Law Reform (Law Com No 293). Retrieved January 10, 2020 from https://s3-eu-west-2.amazonaws.com/lawcom-prod-storage-11jsxou24uy7q/uploads/2015/03/lc293_9th_Programme.pdf

Law Commission of England and Wales. (2006). *Post legislative scrutiny* (October 2006) Cm 6945. Retrieved January 10, 2020 from http://www.lawcom.gov.uk/app/uploads/2015/03/lc302_Post-legislative_Scrutiny.pdf

Levy, R., & Orr, G. (2016). *The law of deliberative democracy*. Routledge.

Liebenberg, S. (2018). Participatory justice in social rights adjudication. *Human Rights Law Review*, 18(4), 623–649. https://doi.org/10.1093/hrlr/ngy028

McKeown, D. (2018). A chronology of same-sex marriage bills introduced into the federal parliament: A quick guide, Research paper series, 2016–17, Parliamentary Library, Canberra, updated February 2018.

Mouawad, S. (2018). Lebanon: Special parliamentary committee on post legislative scrutiny. In F. De Vrieze (Ed.), *Legislative scrutiny: Overview of legislative scrutiny practices in the UK, India, Indonesia and France* (pp. 29–31). Westminster Foundation for Democracy.

Moulds, S. (2016). Committees of influence: Parliamentary committees with the capacity to change Australia's counter-terrorism laws. *Australasian Parliamentary Review*, 31(2), 46–66. https://papers.ssrn.com/sol3/papers.cfm?abstract_id=2934712

Moulds, S. (2019). The role of Commonwealth parliamentary committees in facilitating parliamentary deliberation: A case study of marriage equality reform. In J. Debeljak & L. Grenfell (Eds.), *Law making and human rights* (Chapter 24, pp. 185–230). Thomson Reuters.

Moulds, S. (2019a). Parliamentary rights scrutiny and counter-terrorism lawmaking in Australia. *Journal of Southeast Asian Human Rights*, 3(2), 185–230. https://doi.org/10.19184/jseahr.v3i2.13461

Moulds, S. P. (2018). *The rights protecting role of parliamentary committees: The case of Australia's counter-terrorism laws* [Doctoral dissertation, University of Adelaide]. http://hdl.handle.net/2440/115212

Mulgan, R. (1996). The Australian Senate as a 'House of Review'. *Australian Journal of Political Science*, 31(2), 191–204. https://doi.org/10.1080/10361149651184

Norton. (2005). Debate on constitutional committee's report on 6 June 2005 House of Lords.

Office of the Leader of the House of Commons. (2008). Post-legislative scrutiny – The government's approach. (Stationary Office, March 2008, Cm 7320) 8–9 and 15. Retrieved February 7, 2020 from https://assets.publishing.service.gov.uk/government/uploads/system/uploads/attachment_data/file/228516/7320.pdf

Orr, G., & Levy, R. (2016). Regulating opinion polling: A deliberative democratic perspective. *University of New South Wales Law Journal*, 39(1), 318–340. https://papers.ssrn.com/sol3/papers.cfm?abstract_id=2772419

Parliamentary Joint Committee on Intelligence and Security. (2018). Parliament of Australia, *Advisory Report into the provisions of the Telecommunications and Other Legislation Amendment (Assistance and Access) Bill* 2018 [1.10].

Parliament of Australia (2008). Senate standing committee on legal and constitutional affairs, report on the effectiveness of the sex discrimination act 1984 in eliminating discrimination and promoting gender equality. 12 December 2008, Canberra. https://www.aph.gov.au/Parliamentary_Business/Committees/Senate/Legal_and_Constitutional_Affairs/Completed_inquiries/2008-10/sex_discrim/report/index

Parliament of Australia (2009). Senate standing committee on legal and constitutional affairs, parliament of Australia, inquiry into the marriage equality amendment Bill 2009, (26 November 2009, Canberra). https://www.aph.gov.au/Parliamentary_Business/Committees/Senate/Legal_and_Constitutional_Affairs/Completed_inquiries/2008-10/marriage_equality/index

Parliament of Australia (2012). Senate standing committee on legal and constitutional affairs, Parliament of Australia, inquiry into the marriage equality amendment Bill 2010, (25 June 2012, Canberra), https://www.aph.gov.au/Parliamentary_Business/Committees/Senate/Legal_and_Constitutional_Affairs/Completed_inquiries/2010-13/marriageequality2012/index

Pettit, P. (2001). Deliberative democracy and the case for depoliticising government. *University of New South Wales Law Journal, 24*(3), 724–736. http://classic.austlii.edu.au/au/journals/UNSWLawJl/2001/58.html

Russell, M., & Benton, M. (2009). *Assessing the policy impact of parliament: Methodological challenges and possible future approaches* [Paper presented]. The Public Service Association Legislative Studies Specialist Group Conference, London, United Kingdom, 24 June 2009.

Russell, M., & Gover, D. (2017). *Legislation at Westminster: Parliamentary actors and influence in the making of British law*. Oxford University Press.

Senate Standing Committee on Legal and Constitutional Affairs. (2008, 12 December). *Report on the effectiveness of the sex discrimination act 1984 in eliminating discrimination and promoting gender equality*. Retrieved January 4, 2020 from https://www.aph.gov.au/Parliamentary_Business/Committees/Senate/Legal_and_Constitutional_Affairs/Completed_inquiries/2008-10/sex_discrim/report/index

Sex Discrimination Amendment (Sexual Orientation, Gender Identity and Intersex Status) Act 2013 (Cth).

Sosic, M. (2018). Montenegro: Committee and plenary debate on post legislative scrutiny. In F. De Vrieze (Ed.), *Legislative scrutiny: Overview of legislative scrutiny practices in the UK, India, Indonesia and France* (pp. 26–29). Westminster Foundation for Democracy.

Stephenson, S. (2016). *From dialogue to disagreement in comparative rights constitutionalism*. Federation Press.

Stubbs, M. (2012). A brief history of the judicial review of legislation under the Australian constitution. *Federal Law Review, 40*(2), 227–252. https://doi.org/10.22145/flr.40.2.5

Tolley, M. C. (2009). Parliamentary scrutiny of rights in the United Kingdom: Assessing the work of the joint committee on human rights. *Australian Journal of Political Science, 44*(1), 41–55. https://doi.org/10.1080/10361140802656922

Uhr, J. (1998). *Deliberative democracy in Australia: The changing place of parliament*. Cambridge University Press.

United Kingdom Government, Cabinet Office. (2017). *Guide to Making Legislation*. Retrieved February 7, 2020 from https://www.gov.uk/government/publications/guide-to-making-legislation

Westminster Foundation for Democracy. (2018). *London declaration on post-legislative scrutiny* (online). Retrieved January 10, 2020 from https://www.wfd.org/approach/post-legislative-scrutiny/

Wijananto, A. (2018). Indonesia's legislative scrutiny. In F. De Vrieze (Ed.), *Legislative scrutiny: Overview of legislative scrutiny practices in the UK, India, Indonesia and France* (pp. 22-26). Westminster Foundation for Democracy.

Williams, G., & Burton, L. (2015). Australia's parliamentary scrutiny act: An exclusive parliamentary model of rights protection. In M. Hunt, H. J. Hooper, & P. Yowell (Eds.), *Parliaments and human rights: Redressing the democratic deficit* (pp. 257-277). Hart Publishing.

Williams, G., & Reynolds, D. (2016). The operation and impact of Australia's parliamentary scrutiny regime for human rights. *Monash University Law Review, 41*(2), 469-507. https://www.monash.edu/__data/assets/pdf_file/0006/446181/Vol412_Williams.pdf

The UK post-legislative scrutiny gap

Tom Caygill

ABSTRACT
It is now 10 years since the introduction of the systematic approach to post-legislative scrutiny in the House of Commons and assessments have shown that it is yet to become a regular part of committee work, at least from the perspective of published reports. Although the procedures in the House of Lords are different, the extent of post-legislative scrutiny has also remained limited. This article attempts to identify the post-legislative gap and provides insight into why this gap is occurring. The article begins by analysing the limited amount of post-legislative scrutiny that has taken place to date, before analysing which government departments have been producing post-legislative memoranda and whether these memoranda are being picked up by departmental select committees. In so doing, the article analyses which committees have not, so far, been undertaking post-legislative scrutiny and explores some of the reasons for why they have not engaged.

Introduction

Post-legislative scrutiny is defined by the Law Commission of England and Wales as:

> A broad form of review, the purpose of which is to address the effects of legislation in terms of whether intended policy objectives have been met by the legislation and, if so, how effectively. However this does not preclude consideration of narrow questions of a purely legal or technical nature. (Law Commission, 2006, p. 7)

De Vrieze and Hasson (2017) state that post-legislative scrutiny holds two distinct functions: monitoring of the implementation of legislation and evaluating whether or not the aims of an Act are reflected in the results and effects of legislation once implemented.

In the last decade a more systematic approach has been taken by both government and parliament. With regards to the House of Commons, since 2008, through an agreement between the Committee Office and Cabinet Office, government departments have been required to prepare and publish post-legislative review memoranda, assessing whether an Act of Parliament has met its key objectives, within three to five years of the Act entering the statute books (Kelly & Everett, 2013). These memoranda are then presented to departmental select committees for additional scrutiny. With regards to the House of Lords, in 2012 the Liaison Committee promised to appoint at least one ad hoc committee per session to undertake post-legislative scrutiny on a subject chosen by it (House of Lords Liaison Committee, 2012).

However, it is now 10 years on from the introduction of that systematic approach to post-legislative scrutiny in the House of Commons and as such there is a need to assess this process, from the publication of post-legislative review memoranda through to the undertaking of post-legislative scrutiny by parliamentary committees. Although the procedures in the House of Lords are different, the extent of post-legislative scrutiny has also remained limited. Additionally, while there are patterns emerging of certain committees engaging with post-legislative scrutiny, many do not (at least in terms of holding an inquiry). This article therefore aims to address what limited post-legislative scrutiny has taken place so far and assess what factors if any are affecting the ability and willingness of committees to undertake more post-legislative scrutiny.

It is important to answer the research questions of what the post-legislative gap is, and why a post-legislative gap is occurring on the basis that post-legislative scrutiny is a vital tool which allows parliaments to hold executives to account in terms of the implementation of legislation. Additionally, helping to identify the gap in scrutiny here is also important in understanding the behaviour of committees, particularly in understanding why they do not undertake particular types of scrutiny.

Background

As noted, post-legislative scrutiny is undertaken by two different types of committee in the UK Parliament: departmental select committees in the House of Commons and ad hoc committees in the House of Lords. As such the literature on these two types of committee should give an early indication of how these committees operate and some of the issues that might have an impact on their operation.

Departmental select committees – House of Commons

The Hansard Society (2001), as with other academics such as Longley and Davidson (1998), Shaw (1998) and Strom (1998), regard departmental select committees as the main vehicle for promoting a culture of scrutiny and accountability in the House of Commons. Select committees in the UK undertake a range of 10 core tasks, which were introduced in 2002, of which post-legislative scrutiny is just one (House of Commons Liaison Committee, 2012). The competition between core tasks sees committees focus upon breadth rather than depth in inquiries.

It is 40 years since these sessional committees were created and they still perform an important scrutiny function. Their success in holding the executive accountable comes from the fact that they do not have power over things which greatly matter to government's survival, in comparison with other parliamentary committees in western Europe (Russell & Cowley, 2016). They are therefore treated in a different way to the chamber (Giddings, 1994; Hansard Society, 2001). They set their own agendas (Norton, 2013) and face little meddling in their day-to-day operation from party whips (Russell & Cowley, 2016). There is, however, concern that with extra demands and opportunities placed upon them, committees may no longer be in full control of their own agendas (Brazier & Fox, 2011). They also usually produce reports on a cross-party basis (Russell & Cowley, 2016). The emphasis of these committees was to enhance the role of individual Members of Parliament (MPs) (as opposed to parties) in influencing decision making (Giddings, 1994).

Despite being free to set their own agendas, how and why committees decide which inquiries to undertake and the role the core tasks play in this determination are unclear (Brazier & Fox, 2011). However, there are a number of factors that are likely to play a part in their deliberations, such as the chair, member interest, party balance, political urgency and media interest (Brazier & Fox, 2011).

Recent reforms have increased the importance and influence of select committees; these reforms included the election of committee chairs, which has given them a welcome boost in legitimacy (White, 2015), as well as the election of Members, thereby removing the patronage powers of the whips (Benton & Russell, 2013; Russell, 2013). There has also been an increase in the levels of independence among backbenchers, which has contributed to a greater sense of independence among committees (White, 2015). Such select committees are now flexing their muscles (Crewe, 2015). However, research by Bates et al. (2017) has shown that recent reforms have not had an impact upon the attendance and turnover of Members, which Brazier and Fox (2011) have noted as problematic.

Select/ad hoc committees – House of Lords

The House of Lords was originally a chamber-orientated House, however since the late 1970s it has developed a number of permanent committees alongside a more recent increase in the use of ad hoc committees (Norton, 2013; Rogers & Walters, 2015). Their focus tends to be more cross-cutting than House of Commons committees as they were not created to scrutinise government departments (Norton, 2013). Committees in the House of

Lords tend to focus upon making the best use of the expertise of Members, address cross-cutting issues and complement the work of the Commons (Russell, 2013).

There are, however, some similarities between the two Houses when it comes to committees; the same rules apply to both sets of committees in terms of responses from the government (Rogers & Walters, 2015), and they both operate in a consensual manner (Norton, 2013). However, Russell (2013) argues that the culture of committees in the House of Lords is different from the Commons in the sense that they tend to tackle more strategic and long-term issues and they also tend to have better relationships with government departments (Russell, 2013). Ad hoc committees form an important part of the committee structure in the House of Lords and their usage was expanded in 2012 (House of Lords Liaison Committee, 2012). These committees are only temporary and disband after they have reported, however they allow for detailed scrutiny of government over the course of a year.

Methods

This research took a mixed methods approach. The qualitative element begins with an audit of post-legislative scrutiny. As there was limited data on post-legislative scrutiny, including on the total number of inquiries that have taken place, descriptive data was needed to lay a foundation for the rest of the study. This audit included the collation of data on the number of post-legislative scrutiny inquiries that have taken place, the session, the parliament, the legislation which has received post-legislative scrutiny as well as the committee that had undertaken the scrutiny. Data has also been collated on the number of Acts receiving post-legislative scrutiny in each inquiry and the government under which the legislation was introduced. This data was located from individual committee webpages on the UK Parliament website, from individual post-legislative scrutiny reports as well as from legislation.gov.uk. This data was collected for all post-legislative scrutiny inquiries that took place between 2008 and 2019. Inquiries were determined to be post-legislative scrutiny if the words 'post-legislative scrutiny' appeared in the title, the terms of reference, summary of the report or introduction. Post-legislative scrutiny can be challenging to locate, as this article will address later.

Finally, in terms of quantitative data collection, an audit was also undertaken of post-legislative review memoranda published by government departments. These memoranda were located through searches on the gov.uk website as there is currently no other central depositary where these memoranda are stored. While this might not be the perfect method of detection, it is currently the only way to access them publicly. This data was compiled along departmental lines.

The paper comes to a conclusion with the qualitative elements of this study; this took the form of eight semi-structured interviews from across seven different committees. Five of these committees were from the House of Commons, three of which had undertaken post-legislative scrutiny (Culture, Media and Sport; Health; Justice) and two had not at the time interviews were being undertaken (Education; Work and Pensions). The following criteria were deployed in order to aid selection: the committees have undertaken a formal post-legislative scrutiny inquiry (systematic post-legislative scrutiny); which took place either in the 2010–2015 or the 2015–2017 Parliaments (so that clerks and/or chairs would still be around and the inquiry would not be a too distant memory). The final choices came down to the availability of interviewees and access to committee staff.

Three interviews were undertaken in the House of Lords, two from committees which had undertaken post-legislative scrutiny and one from the House of Lords Liaison Committee, which selects which pieces of legislation go on to receive post-legislative scrutiny. Interviews took place with the clerks of these committees. The same criteria for the selection of House of Commons committees were used here too.

Post-legislative scrutiny undertaken between 2008 and 2017

Table 1 shows that ad hoc committees (in the House of Lords) have undertaken the most post-legislative scrutiny since the start of the 2005 Parliament. This is due to the fact that in 2012 the House of Lords determined that it would create a number of ad hoc committees each session to scrutinise specific issues and that at least one of those committees would be a post-legislative scrutiny committee (House of Lords Liaison Committee, 2012). There was one committee in each session, except in the 2013–2014 session which had two. In terms of the House of Commons, the Justice Committee and the Environment, Food and Rural Affairs Committee have been the most

Table 1. Formal post-legislative scrutiny inquiries by committee.

Committee	Number of inquiries
Ad hoc (House of Lords)	6
Environment, Food and Rural Affairs	3
Justice	3
Digital, Culture, Media and Sport	2
Public Administration and Constitutional Affairs	2
Education	1
Housing, Communities and Local Government	1
Home Affairs	1
Health	1
Joint Committee on Human Rights	1

Source: (www.parliament.uk/committees).

active, with the Digital, Culture, Media and Sport Committee and the Public Administration and Constitutional Affairs Committee coming joint third with two inquiries each over the course of the 11-year period studied.

The other committees in Table 1 have undertaken post-legislative scrutiny once in that time period and not every parliamentary committee is part of the table; indicating they have not undertaken formal post-legislative scrutiny at all during this time period.

Table 2 shows the party of government which introduced the legislation receiving formal post-legislative scrutiny. It shows that 20 out of the 24 Acts which have been subject to formal post-legislative scrutiny were introduced under previous Labour Governments (1964–1970, 1997–2001, 2001–2005, 2005–2010), with only four pieces of legislation being introduced by the 2010–2015 Coalition Government. This can potentially be explained by the fact that the 2008 system encouraged the production of a memorandum, and thus encouraged post-legislative scrutiny, of Acts passed since 2005. During the first half of the 2010 Parliament it would be Labour-introduced legislation which was receiving post-legislative review by the relevant government department. However, we are now well beyond the first half of the 2010 Parliament (Caygill, 2019b). The legislation of the 2010–2015 Coalition Government should now be receiving departmental post-legislative review.

It should also be noted that not all post-legislative scrutiny is driven by memoranda published by government departments under the systematic process, as committees can and do select legislation to receive post-legislative scrutiny without receiving a post-legislative memorandum first. There is no procedural obstacle that could stop committees addressing the legislation of the 2010–2015 Coalition Government. Recent reforms were supposed to have emboldened committees; however, this does not appear to be the case in relation to the selection of legislation to receive post-legislative scrutiny. This suggests that there might be some bias in the selection of legislation that receives post-legislative scrutiny on the basis that some of the legislation of the 2010–2015 Coalition Government now falls into the three-to-five-year timeframe for post-legislative review by a government department. However, the subsequent memoranda from these reviews do not appear to be getting picked up by committees. This raises the question of whether this is a result of the party in government at the time. There may be an unwillingness among MPs from the governing party to subject their own government's legislation to post-legislative scrutiny. The bias here is not completely unexpected as parliament is a political body and as such is going to act in a political way. It is key, however, for parliament and especially committees to be aware of these inherent biases over selection and work to address them.

Table 2. Legislation receiving formal post-legislative scrutiny by party of government.

Committee	Session	No of Acts scrutinised	Act(s) involved	Party of government
Environment, Food and Rural Affairs	2007/08	1	Veterinary Surgeons Act 1966	Labour
Digital, Culture, Media and Sport	2008/09	1	Licensing Act 2003	Labour
Ad hoc (Lords)	2012/13	2	Adoption and Children Act 2002; Children and Adoption Act 2006	Labour
Digital, Culture, Media and Sport	2012/13	1	Gambling Act 2005	Labour
Justice	2012/13	1	Freedom of Information Act 2000	Labour
Public Administration and Constitutional Affairs	2012/13	1	Statistics and Registration Service Act 2007	Labour
Ad hoc (Lords)	2013/14	1	Inquiries Act 2005	Labour
Ad hoc (Lords)	2013/14	1	Mental Capacity Act 2005	Labour
Health	2013/14	1	Mental Health Act 2007	Labour
Housing, Communities and Local Government	2013/14	1	Greater London Authority Act 2007	Labour
Joint Committee on Human Rights	2013/14	1	Terrorism Prevention and Investigation Measures Act 2011	Conservative/Liberal Democrat
Justice	2013/14	1	Serious Crime Act 2007	Labour
Public Administration and Constitutional Affairs	2013/14	1	Charities Act 2006	Labour
Ad hoc (Lords)	2014/15	1	Extradition Act 2003	Labour
Home Affairs	2014/15	1	Regulation of Investigatory Powers Act 2000	Labour
Justice	2014/15	1	Legal Aid, Sentencing and Punishment Act 2012	Conservative/Liberal Democrat
Ad hoc (Lords)	2015/16	1	Equality Act 2010	Labour
Ad hoc (Lords)	2016/17	1	Licensing Act 2003	Labour
Environment, Food and Rural Affairs	2016/17	1	Animal Welfare Act 2006	Labour
Environment, Food and Rural Affairs	2016/17	1	Flood and Water Management Act 2010	Labour
Ad hoc (Lords)	2017/19	1	Natural Environment and Rural Communities Act 2006	Labour
Ad hoc (Lords)	2017/19	1	Bribery Act 2010	Labour
Education	2017/19	1	Children and Families Act 2014	Conservative/Liberal Democrat
Ad hoc (Lords)	2017/19	1	Electoral Administration and Registration Act 2013	Conservative/Liberal Democrat

Source: (www.parliament.uk/committees; www.legislation.gov.uk).

The post-legislative gap: selection of legislation

In the previous section, the selection of legislation was addressed and in particular the party which introduced it. It showed that there is something of a party bias when it comes to the selection of legislation, with legislation introduced by the 2010–2015 Coalition Government not yet receiving much attention when it comes to post-legislative scrutiny, with only four Acts having been reviewed so far. There is clearly a gap here in the coverage of post-legislative scrutiny, especially if you consider that government departments are now required to complete their own post-legislative review three to five years after an Act has entered the statue books. This could be more accurately referred to as a post-legislative gap (ie what legislation is not receiving post-legislative scrutiny). While the government process appears to be systematic, the parliament side of it is less so.

At the time of writing, taking into account the three-to-five-year post-legislative departmental review process, committees, as long as departments are producing their reviews on time, should now have received the reviews for the first three sessions of the 2010 Parliament (2010–2012; 2012–2013; 2013–2014). This is assuming that government departments take the full five years to produce the review. The Head of the House of Commons Scrutiny Unit noted that they tend to come towards the end of the given time period because of other departmental priorities (Interview with the Head of the House of Commons Scrutiny Unit). That totals 102 pieces of legislation[1] that should have received their departmental reviews and only four pieces of that legislation have received post-legislative scrutiny (4 per cent).

In terms of the lack of post-legislative scrutiny on the Coalition Government's legislation in the House of Lords, this might be explained by the longer timeframe the Lords likes to take when undertaking post-legislative scrutiny. Interviews with clerks in the House of Lords pointed to a period of time greater than five years needing to pass before legislation is deemed suitable to undertake post-legislative scrutiny on an Act (Caygill, 2019a). The Clerk of the Licensing Act 2003 Committee suggested that seven to eight years would need to pass before it was possible to see the full effects of the Act (Interview with the Clerk of the Licensing Act 2003 Committee). This was on the basis that not all of the Act necessarily comes into force at the same time. Indeed, this view was shared by the Clerk of the House of Lords Liaison Committee, who stated that the optimal time for post-legislative scrutiny is somewhere between 5 and 10 years (Interview with the Clerk of the House of Lords Liaison Committee). This would potentially explain why the House of Lords has not addressed much legislation passed by the 2010–2015 Coalition Government, if it is taking that long-term view. Although that particular reason, 10 years on from the formation of the 2010–2015 Coalition Government, is losing what strength it has.

Table 3. Departmental select committees which have not undertaken a formal post-legislative scrutiny inquiry.

Committees
Business, Energy and Industrial Strategy Committee
Defence Committee
Foreign Affairs Committee
International Development Committee
Northern Ireland Affairs Committee
Scottish Affairs Committee
Transport Committee
Treasury Committee
Welsh Affairs Committee
Work and Pensions Committee

In justifying this longer term view the Clerk of the Equality Act 2010 Committee noted that '3 years is too short a time as you can't really see what an Act is doing, what has been achieved and what hasn't' (Interview with the Clerk of the Equality Act 2010 Committee). So while the government focuses upon the date of royal assent, it might, in fact, be better to focus upon the date of commencement, as the House of Lords Constitution Committee (2004) does. In relation to this point he raised the case of the Licensing Act 2003, which the House of Commons Culture, Media and Sport Committee scrutinised just three years after the Act had come into force. The report ended up being short, on the basis that there was not much to say other than noting that it was too soon after the Act had been passed to make any concrete suggestions (Interview with the Clerk of the Equality Act 2010 Committee). The House of Lords assessed the legislation again in the 2016/2017 session, 11 years after its enactment on the statute books.

From the perspective of the House of Commons, the former Clerk of the Culture, Media and Sport Committee noted that there is a tendency to put at least a parliament (around five years) between the legislation being passed and the undertaking of post-legislative scrutiny. She also noted that it is possible that a timeframe of seven to eight years would be necessary depending upon the policy area in question (Interview with the former Clerk of the Culture, Media and Sport Committee).

The post-legislative gap: House of Commons committees and UK Government

Post-legislative gap does not just appear in terms of the legislation selected for post-legislative scrutiny. There is also a post-legislative gap in terms of the committees that have not undertaken formal post-legislative scrutiny since 2010.

Table 3 shows the House of Commons departmental select committees that have not undertaken a formal post-legislative scrutiny inquiry since 2010. The

Foreign Affairs, International Development, Defence and the Northern Ireland, Scottish and Welsh Affairs committees can be excused to some degree as these departments are not as legislatively intensive in comparison with the others. Additionally, the Treasury Committee could also be excused to a limited degree because financial legislation is currently not eligible for post-legislative scrutiny under the government's agreement with parliament, nor was it deemed eligible by the House of Lords Constitution Committee (House of Lords Select Committee on the Constitution, 2004; Office of the Leader of the House of Commons, 2008). Nevertheless, the core tasks of departmental select committees are relevant to all departmental select committees, of which post-legislative scrutiny is one of those tasks. That leaves an additional three committees which have not undertaken a formal post-legislative scrutiny inquiry. While it might be expected that the party of the chair might have an impact here, half of the committees which did not undertake any post-legislative scrutiny between 2010 and 2019 have had opposition chairs and half have had government chairs and as such there does not appear to be a trend.

However, when assessing the post-legislative memoranda published by government departments, Figure 1 raises a number of issues. First, the Home Office has published far more memoranda than the Home Affairs Committee has taken up for post-legislative scrutiny. While not all legislation will require scrutiny, with the Home Affairs Committee having only undertaken one inquiry in comparison with 18 memoranda having been published, it again shows that post-legislative scrutiny is not systematic. Additionally, for each of the committees listed in the previous paragraph for not having undertaken any post-legislative scrutiny, all of their respective departments (except

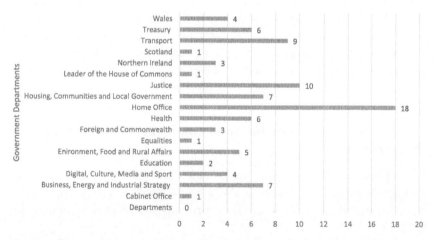

Figure 1. Post-legislative memoranda published by government departments. Source: gov.uk.

International Development and Defence)[2] have been publishing memoranda, albeit some more than others.

Ninety-one post-legislative memoranda were published by government departments between 2008 and 2019. This is some way below the amount of legislation that went on to receive royal assent in the same time period. For instance, between the 2010–2012 and 2013–2014 sessions 102 pieces of legislation received royal assent, however only 11 of them (11 per cent) have received their post-legislative review memoranda. Eight of those were on government bills and three on private members bills.[3] This suggests that while there is a problem with committees picking up memoranda (and they do not need a memo to launch an inquiry) there is also a problem at the government end in terms of publishing these memoranda.

Figure 2 shows a steady increase in the undertaking and publication of post-legislative review memoranda up until 2012, however since then it has declined to single figures each year.[4] It was between 2011 and 2014 when most memoranda were published; perhaps it is not surprising that in this time period it is Labour-introduced legislation that will be within the timeframe for post-legislative review. It has been highlighted that there is some bias in the selection of legislation (Caygill, 2019b), however perhaps there is a bias in relation to government departments as well; particularly as we see the number of memoranda decline as Coalition legislation reaches the point of requiring review. This will also be having an impact upon the selection of legislation by committees for post-legislative scrutiny as these memoranda act as a trigger for committees (Caygill, 2019a). There is an additional factor

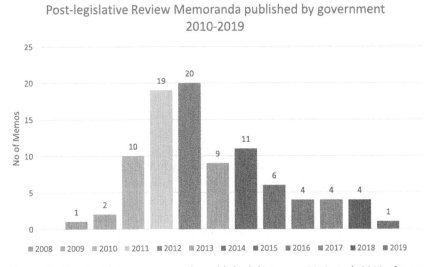

Figure 2. Post-legislative memoranda published between 2010 and 2019. Source: gov.uk.

affecting the 2017 to mid-2019 period and that is the pressure that the UK's exit from the European Union is putting on government departments (eg staff being loaned from other departments to the Department for Exiting the European Union) (Owens & Lloyd, 2018); it is conceivable that post-legislative review has fallen off departmental radars. It is currently not known how much encouragement there is in relation to post-legislative scrutiny between the Cabinet Office and other government departments. In their 'Guide to Making Legislation' (published in 2017) the Cabinet Office reaffirmed their commitment to the 2008 agreement and made clear that the responsibility for undertaking post-legislative review was with respective government departments but made no mention of enforcement mechanisms. The lack of an enforcement mechanism within parliament only adds to the fact that there does not appear to be a commitment from the Cabinet Office to oversee the process within government either. Until such an enforcement mechanism exists, post-legislative scrutiny is likely to continue to fall off the radar of both government departments as well as House of Commons committees.

The post-legislative gap: case studies

In order to understand why this post-legislative gap is occurring interviews were undertaken with the clerks of two House of Commons committees which had not engaged with post-legislative scrutiny at the time that interviews were undertaken. These committees were the Education Committee and the Work and Pension Committee. In terms of the Education Committee, the clerk noted that they came very close to launching a post-legislative scrutiny inquiry into the Children and Families Act 2014 but due to the surprise calling of the 2017 general election this inquiry did not proceed (Interview with the former Clerk of the Education Committee). A version of this inquiry has since taken place, and the report was published just before the 2019 general election. So there was a problem here of events taking over. This can be both political events such as elections halting committee work or even new policy announcements which divert the attention of the committee away from tasks such as post-legislative scrutiny. However, it appears that post-legislative scrutiny was on their agenda even if only lower down it. In terms of the Work and Pension Committee, attention is paid to what is likely to be published by the department in terms of post-legislative memoranda and discussions are held about what if anything the committee would like to move forward with, but the committee does not usually make much further progress than that (Interview with the former Clerk of the Work and Pensions Committee). These factors only add to the list of factors that affect committee work programmes, which Geddes (2020, pp. 99–101) notes.

There is also the potential for committee work programmes to be overtaken by parliamentary and legislative cycles, in the sense that once one bill has been passed work starts on the next (Interview with the former Clerk of the Education Committee). There is then a conveyer belt of legislation, which (a) undertakes some of its own post-legislative review in terms of looking back at the previous Act and amending it through a new one and (b) means post-legislative scrutiny does not take place as the legislation is not on the statute books long enough before the next piece of legislation comes along and supersedes it. The former Clerk of the House of Commons Education Committee noted that the Department for Education had been in a state of permanent revolution since 2010, with a near constant cycle of legislation coming out of the department. This means there is plenty of material to look at potentially but also makes the job of undertaking post-legislative scrutiny more challenging if it is superseding earlier laws. It also potentially eliminates some legislation from the running for post-legislative scrutiny. This problem was also raised in relation to the Work and Pensions Committee, in that nearly every year a new Pensions Bill appears, potentially superseding or dealing with the challenges presented in the previous Act. As a result, the government department does not undertake a formal post-legislative scrutiny review as it claims it reviewed the legislation when crafting the new bill (Interview with the former Clerk of the Work and Pensions Committee). This might partially explain the low number of post-legislative review memoranda arriving for Coalition legislation, however an equally compelling explanation would be that government departments are being overwhelmed by Brexit and as such post-legislative review is even further down the agenda than usual.

This does come down to power, to some extent, as the power to pull together and produce these memoranda rests with the government, not parliament. Although parliament can call for papers they rely upon government for their production and for the information contained within them. While parliament has little or no coercive powers, it is also left weaker by being at an informational and resource disadvantage to government. Access to information is a vital foundation for all scrutiny, and the government-led focus in terms of post-legislative scrutiny memoranda could be a limitation to wanting to undertake it in the first place. In terms of power in this situation, parliament often relies upon convention and the creation of an obligation, and commitment from government, what Lukes (1974) would term persuasion or manipulation. Boulding (1989), in *Three Faces of Power*, refers to this as the kiss. Although, as the parliamentary reform literature notes, the government will be in no hurry to change this face and alter the balance of power (Kelso, 2009). It should be noted that it is not unusual to see bodies internal to legislatures undertaking this kind of review, which is currently undertaken by the executive in the UK (De Vrieze & Hasson, 2017).

That being said, both clerks argued that their committees had undertaken post-legislative scrutiny in other ways (Interview with the former Clerk of the Education Committee; Interview with the former Clerk of the Work and Pensions Committee). For the Education Committee, this included a number of sessions they had on the work of the Children's Commissioner for England, which the clerk argued had a clear and demonstrable link to the Children and Families Act 2014. In relation to the Work and Pensions Committee, the former Clerk argued that they did a lot of work that was driven by politics and driven by constituency mailbag issues. Geddes (2020) also noted that constituency experience can drive select committee inquiries and this ties in with his typology of styles of scrutiny (eg constituency champions who represent their constituents in the topics they pursue). One of those issues related to the state pension age and the Women Against State Pension Inequality (WASPI) campaign. It was a very high profile politically driven inquiry and, in practice, a lot of what they focused upon was tantamount to looking at the legislation and whether it was achieving its objectives or whether policy was enacted in the way it ought to have been (Interview with the former Clerk of Work and Pensions Committee). He argued that a lot of it was about communication and it bore quite a lot of the hallmarks of a post-legislative scrutiny inquiry. He also noted that he did not think anyone involved was consciously thinking that at the time. However, in hindsight, you could see it in those terms (Interview with the former Clerk of the Work and Pensions Committee). This highlights the issue that perhaps post-legislative scrutiny is being undertaken in a variety of forms, aside from a formal committee inquiry, which might not be detectable at first glance. Care is required here however; these alternative forms have not yet been mapped out and caution should be taken in classifying them as post-legislative scrutiny. That being said, the Law Commission in its 2006 report on post-legislative scrutiny noted that more systematic post-legislative scrutiny could take different forms (Law Commission, 2006), the problem is we do not yet know what these different forms are. This emphasises the need for additional research into alternative forms of post-legislative scrutiny, particularly as both clerks noted the challenges in identifying where post-legislative scrutiny has taken place.

The former Clerk of the Education Committee also noted a problem of Members' interest in relation to post-legislative scrutiny and the potential lack of interest. Indeed, the former Clerk of the Work and Pensions Committee argued that post-legislative scrutiny is often way down on the list of priorities of Members, and because they only maybe spend a couple of hours a week on committee work it never rises much higher on the list of priorities. Indeed, a survey undertaken by the Hansard Society in 2011 found that MPs spent only 14 per cent of their time on committee work (Korris, 2011). This is in comparison with 21 per cent of time being spent in the chamber and 59 per cent spent on constituency-related issues (campaigning, casework and meetings) (Korris, 2011). The Clerk of the House of Commons Education Committee argued that interest in the study or review of legislation and the legislative process is probably restricted to the Members who are lawyers or who are more technically minded (Interview with the former Clerk of the Education Committee); these kinds of MP would be referred to as 'specialists' under Geddes (2020) typology. The former Clerk of the Education Committee suggested that they would never refer to an inquiry as post-legislative scrutiny as it was a sure way to turn off Members and potentially miss an opportunity for public engagement (Interview with the former Clerk of the Education Committee). Instead, he noted that mentions of post-legislative scrutiny would be placed in the terms of reference so that witnesses would understand how to approach the inquiry.

There is also an additional problem raised by the former Clerk of the Work and Pensions Committee which has had an impact upon the Work and Pensions Committee at least, and that is in relation to the turnover of committee membership. Data from the Institute for Government shows that turnover on the Work and Pensions Committee in the 2010–2015 Parliament was over 150 per cent, which will have had a big impact upon the dynamic and interests of the Committee (Freeguard, 2015). That being said, the Justice Committee was active in terms of undertaking post-legislative scrutiny during the 2010 Parliament but had a turnover of just over 140 per cent (Freeguard, 2015). The Chair of the Justice Committee at the time, however, was committed to undertaking post-legislative scrutiny (Interview with Lord Beith, former Chair of the Justice Committee), which will have had an impact upon its prevalence here despite the turnover in Members. Turnover might not be the most important factor when determining whether to undertake post-legislative scrutiny, but if a chair is ambivalent to it, turnover is unlikely to help push it up the agenda. The clerk argued that you may at the start of a parliament plan to address a particular Act a few years down the line but if a number of Members change (including those with the desire to do it) then that can cause a change to the work programme via Members' priorities (Interview with the former Clerk of the House of Commons Work and Pensions Committee). This potentially ties in with events discussed earlier and a high membership turnover makes planning and sticking to a long-term work programme more challenging. Members' interest is important here in determining committee behaviour but also in terms of new Members' interests as they join committees and dilute the earlier interests.

Conclusion

Post-legislative scrutiny remains limited as a form of scrutiny, at least from the perspective of committees launching inquiries and publishing reports. From the limited amount of post-legislative scrutiny that has taken place it is possible to locate a gap or rather a post-legislative scrutiny gap. This gap appears both in terms of the selection of legislation (in particular through a lack of selection of legislation passed by the 2010–2015 Coalition Government onwards), and in terms of committees in the House of Commons which are not undertaking post-legislative scrutiny despite post-legislative review memoranda being published across almost the full range of government departments. However, there is now a post-legislative scrutiny gap created through a slowdown in the number of reviews coming out of government departments. Although not all inquiries are launched because of post-legislative review memos, they do act as a prompt for committees to undertake post-legislative scrutiny. Putting the 2008 agreement between the Commons Committee Office and Cabinet Office on to firmer footage would probably help increase the production and take-up of memoranda. The Liaison Committees of both Houses of Parliament would be a suitable unit to provide some parliamentary oversight of the process.

However, there are a number of reasons why committees might not be formally engaging with post-legislative scrutiny. These include events taking over. These can be both political events such as elections halting committee work or new policy announcements which divert the attention of the committee away from tasks such as post-legislative scrutiny. There is also the problem of committee work programmes being overtaken by legislative cycles. There is often a conveyer belt of legislation, which undertakes some of its own post-legislative review in terms of looking back at the previous Act and amending it through a new one. This often means that post-legislative scrutiny does not take place as the legislation is not on the statute books long enough to receive a post-legislative memorandum or before the next piece of legislation comes along and supersedes it. In addition, there was a problem with long-term planning due to the turnover of committee membership. Turnover might not be the most important factor when determining whether to undertake post-legislative scrutiny, but if a chair is ambivalent to it, turnover is unlikely to help push it up the agenda. Finally, there is also a lack of Member interest in post-legislative scrutiny, and with member-driven committees interest is vital.

Notes

1. Not including financial legislation.
2. The Department for Exiting the European Union and the Department for International Trade have been excluded from this study on the basis that their legislation is not eligible for post-legislative scrutiny.
3. Post-legislative scrutiny has not yet been undertaken on private members' bills.
4. The years 2016, 2017 and 2018 each include one memorandum requested by the House of Lords Liaison Committee for scrutiny by an ad hoc committee, therefore are not officially part of the three-to-five-year timeframe set out by the government and the House of Commons.

Acknowledgements

The author wishes to thank attendees at the PSA Annual Conference 2019 and the ECPR General Conference 2019 as well as colleagues at Newcastle University for their helpful comments on earlier drafts of this research.

Disclosure statement

No potential conflict of interest was reported by the author(s).

Funding

This work was supported by the Economic and Social Research Council [Grant number ES/J500082/1].

References

Bates, S., Goodwin, M., & McKay, S. (2017). Do UK MPs engage more with select committees since the wright reforms? An interrupted time series analysis, 1979–2016. *Parliamentary Affairs*, 70(1), 780–800. https://doi.org/10.1093/pa/gsx007

Benton, M., & Russell, M. (2013). Assessing the impact of parliamentary oversight committees: The select committees in the British House of Commons. *Parliamentary Affairs*, 66(4), 772–797. https://doi.org/10.1093/pa/gss009

Boulding, K. (1989). *Three faces of power*. Sage.

Brazier, A., & Fox, R. (2011). Reviewing select committee tasks and modes of operation. *Parliamentary Affairs*, 64(2), 354–369. https://doi.org/10.1093/pa/gsr007

Caygill, T. (2019a). A tale of two houses? Post-legislative scrutiny in the UK parliament. *European Journal of Law Reform*, 21(2), 5–19. https://doi.org/10.5553/EJLR/138723702019021002002

Caygill, T. (2019b). Legislation under review: An assessment of post-legislative scrutiny recommendations in the UK parliament. *The Journal of Legislative Studies*, 25(2), 295–313. https://doi.org/10.1080/13572334.2019.1603260

Crewe, E. (2015). *The House of Commons: An anthropology of MPs at work*. Bloomsbury Academic.

De Vrieze, F., & Hasson, V. (2017). *Post-legislative scrutiny: Comparative study of practices of post-legislative scrutiny in selected parliaments and the rationale for its place in democracy assistance*. Westminster Foundation for Democracy.

Freeguard, G. (2015). Members' exits – And entrances: select committee membership, 2010–15 [Online]. Institute for Government. Retrieved June 5, 2018 from https://www.instituteforgovernment.org.uk/blog/members%E2%80%99-exits-%E2%80%93-and-entrances-select-committee-membership-2010-15

Geddes, M. (2020). *Dramas at Westminster*. Manchester University Press.

Giddings, P. (1994). Select committees and parliamentary scrutiny: Plus Ça change. *Parliamentary Affairs*, 47(4), 669–686. https://doi.org/10.1093/oxfordjournals.pa.a052504

Hansard Society. (2001). *The challenge for parliament: Making government accountable: Report of the Hansard Society commission on parliamentary scrutiny.*

House of Lords Liaison Committee. (2012). *Review of select committee activity and proposals for new committee activity.* 21st March 2012. HL 279. 2010-12.

House of Lords Select Committee on the Constitution. (2004). *Parliament and the legislative process.* 29th October 2004. HL 173-I. 2003–2004.

Kelly, R., & Everett, M. (2013). *Post-legislative scrutiny.* House of Commons Library Standard Note. SN/PC/05232. 23rd May 2013.

Kelso, A. (2009). *Parliamentary reform at Westminster.* Manchester University Press.

Korris, M. (2011). *A year in the life: From member of public to member of parliament: Interim briefing paper.* Hansard Society.

Law Commission. (2006). *Post-legislative scrutiny.* October 2006. Cm 6945.

Longley, L. D., & Davidson, R. H. (1998). Parliamentary committees: Changing perspectives on changing institutions. *The Journal of Legislative Studies*, 4(2), 1–20. https://doi.org/10.1080/13572339808420537

Lukes, S. (1974). *Power: A radical view.* MacMillan.

Norton, P. (2013). *Parliament in British politics* (2nd ed.). Palgrave MacMillan.

Office of the Leader of the House of Commons. (2008). *Post-legislative scrutiny – The Government's approach.* March 2008. Cm 7320.

Owens, J., & Lloyd, L. (2018). Costing brexit: What is Whitehall spending on exiting the EU?. Institute for Government. Retrieved May 29, 2019 from https://www.instituteforgovernment.org.uk/sites/default/files/publications/cost-of-brexit-what-whitehall-spending-insight-final-vb_1.pdf

Rogers, R., & Walters, R. (2015). *How parliament works* (7th ed.). Routledge.

Russell, M. (2013). *The contemporary House of Lords.* Oxford University Press.

Russell, M., & Cowley, P. (2016). The policy power of the Westminster parliament: The "parliamentary state" and the empirical evidence. *Governance*, 29(1), 121–137. https://doi.org/10.1111/gove.12149

Shaw, M. (1998). Parliamentary committees: A global perspective. *The Journal of Legislative Studies*, 4(1), 225–251. https://doi.org/10.1080/13572339808420547

Strom, K. (1998). Parliamentary committees in European democracies. *The Journal of Legislative Studies*, 4(1), 21–59. https://doi.org/10.1080/13572339808420538

White, H. (2015). *Select committees under scrutiny.* Institute for Government.

Ex-post evaluation in the European Parliament: an increasing influence on the policy cycle

Irmgard Anglmayer ⓘ* and Amandine Scherrer*

ABSTRACT
The European Parliament has institutionalised its use of ex-post evaluation in the wake of the EU Better Regulation agenda. This article explores the nature, function and impact of the European Parliament's evaluations. It briefly sets out its characteristic dual structure, which combines a political committee report with a technical supporting study drawn up by Parliament's research service. It then reflects on the manifold purposes of parliamentary evaluation. Thereby, particular attention is paid to policy learning and agenda setting. There is evidence that Parliament's evaluations have, in some cases, been able to influence the agenda for the revision of existing EU legislation. This is supported by two case studies that demonstrate the European Parliament's increasing role and capacity to impact the European Commission's policy cycle. The first relates to the Directive on cross-border mergers and divisions, and the second to citizenship and residency by investment schemes ('golden visas' and 'golden passports').

The context: ex-post evaluation in parliaments across the EU

Over recent decades, the importance of evaluation has grown globally. Academics deem evaluation a 'booming business' (Leeuw, 2009) arguing that 'evaluation is becoming a taken-for-granted aspect of policy-making' (Dahler-Larsen, 2007, p. 142). Generally, an institutionalisation of policy evaluation can be observed (Jacob et al., 2015), including within the European Union (EU). Almost all EU Member States, plus the EU itself (as a supranational organisation), have put ex-post mechanisms in place to assess the effectiveness, continued relevance and administrative burdens of existing legislation and policies.

This increasing institutionalisation of evaluation across the European Union has benefited from a move, at global level, to develop regulatory

---

*Both authors are writing in a personal capacity and any views expressed do not represent an official position of the Parliament or the EBA.

policy and governance. For EU countries, a key facilitator in this process was a recommendation put forward by the Organisation for Economic Co-operation and Development (OECD) in 2012.[1] The OECD recommendation, endorsed by most EU countries,[2] calls on governments to review their regulatory stock systematically. However, a recent comparative OECD report shows that, across the EU, evaluation is predominantly conducted at the level of the executive, and is, as yet, far less developed in parliamentary settings (OECD, 2019).[3]

A similar conclusion is reached in the 2015 update of the 'International atlas of evaluation' (Jacob et al., 2015) which examined, inter alia, parliaments' performance of active and passive evaluation. Overall, the atlas establishes that the institutionalisation of evaluation in parliaments is rather weak in general, including in the EU countries examined.[4] Thus, despite the observed general rise in evaluation, the specific role of ex-post evaluation in parliaments appears to be only emerging.

A recent survey-based study by the European Parliamentary Research Service draws a slightly more optimistic picture (Anglmayer, 2020). It finds that, while virtually all EU national parliaments avail of tools to passively scrutinise the implementation of laws (e.g. in sectoral committees, hearings, plenary debates or by means of questions or interpellations), active ex-post evaluation remains limited to roughly one third of parliaments. These are notably the parliaments of Belgium, France, Italy, Poland, Sweden and the United Kingdom (UK);[5] and, on a smaller scale, also Bulgaria, Latvia and the Netherlands. Some of them have a long-standing tradition of policy evaluation (e.g. France and Sweden), while others (e.g. Bulgaria, Italy and Latvia) have built their evaluation capacities much more recently.

Against this background and compared with most EU national parliaments, the degree of institutionalisation evaluation gained in the European Parliament (EP) appears rather high. A dedicated evaluation system has been put in place in recent years (since 2014, to be precise), which, despite its 'youth', appears to stand out amidst the EU parliamentary landscape. This system, set up together with dedicated ex-ante impact assessment capacities, reflects Parliament's commitment to the principle of evidence-based policy-making.

At the end of Parliament's legislative term 2014–2019, it seems worthwhile to reflect on the nature, function and merits of the EP's evaluation system, and to draw some preliminary conclusions on the evidence regarding its potential for influencing the EU policy cycle.

This article[6] first briefly depicts the EP evaluation system, with a particular focus on its characteristic dual structure (Chapter 2). It then reflects on the manifold purposes of policy evaluation in parliaments, thereby paying special attention to the evaluation purposes of the European Parliament, in particular accountability, transparency, policy learning and – last but not least – agenda setting (Chapter 3). The fourth chapter details how parliamentary committees use supporting research studies for decision-making and how Parliament's evaluation work has fed into the European Commission's policy work, thus influencing the policy cycle. This is illustrated by two case studies: the EP evaluation of the Directive on cross-border mergers and divisions and the study examining the 'golden visas' and 'golden passport' schemes.

Ex-post evaluation at the European Parliament

The Lisbon Treaty and the Better Regulation agenda paving the way

Zooming in on the EU institutions, the European Parliament has begun to assume an increasingly important role in evaluation in recent years, as part of its general oversight function over the executive. However, this does not alter the fact that the European Commission – the executive – remains the main evaluator of EU policies and legislation, in view of its particular role as 'the guardian of the Treaties'. Compared with Parliament, where committees are free to select files ad hoc for ex-post evaluation, according to their priorities and political agenda, the Commission has a broad and systemic obligation to evaluate the transposition and implementation of EU law, policies and spending programmes (Rufas Quintana & Anglmayer, 2019). In particular, the Commission's evaluations are triggered most often through evaluation clauses included in the legal acts themselves, financial requirements, or the EU Better Regulation agenda. However, even if the triggers for evaluation may be different in the two institutions, their purpose is the same: they mainly serve to assess if the stock of EU regulation remains fit for purpose.

The EP institutionalised the use of ex-post evaluation (together with ex-ante impact assessment) during the course of its eighth legislative term (2014–2019). Two factors paved the way for this development:

(1) The power gained through the Treaty of Lisbon, in force since December 2009. This made the EP a fully-fledged parliament, boosting its confidence as co-legislator and scrutiniser. In this context, the Treaty change prompted Parliament to shift its law-making focus from a narrow approach (the deliberations in the legislative phase, i.e. the time window between the reception of the legislative proposal and the adoption of the legal act), to a much broader one, encompassing a keen interest in legislative agenda-setting and ex-post scrutiny, next to law-making in the strict sense.
(2) The EU's Better Regulation agenda, which is broadly speaking the EU's framework for evidence-based policy-making, to which the EP is firmly committed. In this context, a 2011 EP resolution[7] led to the establishment

of a dedicated impact assessment capacity within the EP administration (covering both ex-ante impact assessment and ex-post evaluation). Moreover, the 2016 Interinstitutional Agreement on Better Law-Making,[8] which includes a reinforced commitment to ex-post evaluation (paragraphs 20–24), forms the compass of the three institutions' respective roles and action throughout the entire law-making process.

Formal versus informal evaluation in parliaments

In general, parliaments are 'not themselves among the big producers of evaluations' (Jacob et al., 2015, p. 19). As stated above, only few parliaments actively engage in this area EU-wide, conducting their own ex-post reviews. Moreover, those who do engage are highly selective in the files to cover and do not conduct evaluations in large quantities (Anglmayer, 2020). One reason for the observed restrained parliamentary engagement in carrying out their own evaluations may be that, compared to the executive, parliaments often lack capacities in terms of resources and infrastructure (Auel, 2017).

The few national parliaments that do engage in ex-post evaluation have either a system in place at administrative level (e.g. parliamentary research service or other dedicated entity) or at the level of parliamentary committees or other formal structures composed by Members of Parliament. The former has been referred to in literature as 'informal scrutiny' and the latter as 'formal scrutiny' (Griglio, 2019). It appears important to distinguish between these levels with regard to the systems' political powerfulness.

Italy provides an example of a parliament conducting 'informal scrutiny',[9] with its Service for Parliamentary Oversight in the Chamber of Deputies, and its recently set-up Office for Impact Assessment in the Senate. Both administrative entities scrutinise the implementation of law. However, regardless of the depth and quality of these administrative evaluation reports, from a political perspective, this instrument appears weak, as it does 'not automatically trigger any procedural follow-up' (Griglio, 2019).

In contrast, the parliaments of Belgium, Sweden, France and the UK have structures in place for 'formal scrutiny' (Anglmayer, 2020; and Griglio, 2019). In Belgium, the joint Committee for Legislative Monitoring *(Comité parlementaire chargé du suivi législatif / Parlementair Comité belast met de wetsevaluatie)*, composed of Members from both chambers, conducts evaluations. It can present a proposal for a legislative revision to both chambers.[10]

In France and in Sweden, parliament's power to conduct ex-post evaluation is constitutionally anchored. The French Parliament entrusts evaluation to the standing committees, and additionally can set up specific ad hoc bodies for evaluation purposes. In the National Assembly, the Committee for Public Policy Evaluation and Control *(Comité d'évaluation et de contrôle des politiques publiques; CEC)* delivers cross-cutting evaluations. The CEC evaluation findings are usually debated in plenary, but not voted. In Sweden, evaluations are carried out by standing committees, supported by committee secretariats and a dedicated research unit[11] within the *Riksdag* administration. *Riksdag* evaluations are formally transmitted to all concerned public authorities for follow-up.

Finally, in the UK parliament, departmental select committees in the House of Commons may choose acts for ex-post evaluation. Conversely, the House of Lords can appoint ad hoc committees to undertake post-legislative scrutiny. These Lords committees however dissolve immediately after the publication of their report, which appears to hamper an effective follow-up (Caygill, 2019).

Both, formal and informal evaluation systems have their advantages and disadvantages. Formal scrutiny, carried out by parliamentary committees or similar structures composed of Members, can be a politically strong oversight tool, since, depending on the national framework, such committees may be vested with the power to require follow-up action from the executive. Furthermore, they can adopt formal documents expressing the view of the committee or even the parliament itself (e.g. adopted resolutions), which may attract public attention and media coverage. In comparison, informal scrutiny by means of evaluation studies drawn up by dedicated administrative services of parliaments may go into more depth. They are impartial and ideally grounded on sound methodology. Nevertheless, from a political perspective, they constitute a softer oversight tool, since they can only address shortcomings and make recommendations, whilst they have no formal power to require a follow-up from the executive (Griglio, 2019). They are usually not formally submitted to government.

The dual mechanism of a political report/resolution and a technical study

Compared with the parliamentary evaluation systems of EU Member States briefly sketched out above, the European Parliament avails of a system that combines both features, formal and informal scrutiny. This two-faceted system consists of two interlinked tools:

First and foremost, an EP evaluation report ('implementation report')[12] drawn up by the competent standing committee, which is then voted in plenary; and second, an impartial, factual evaluation study drafted by a dedicated evaluation unit within parliament's administration. This unit is part of the European Parliamentary Research Service (EPRS). The study, termed 'European Implementation Assessment' (EIA), is intended to strengthen the evidence base of the implementation report.

Strictly speaking, implementation reports are not restricted to examining the implementation of EU legislation, but have a broader mandate. According to the rules in place, their subjects can be 'transposition into national law, implementation and enforcement of the Treaties and other Union legislation, soft law instruments and international agreements'.[13] While the use of implementation reports can be traced back to 2008 (Corbett et al., 2016, p. 319), a strategic and routine use of this instrument has emerged only in the current parliamentary term, i.e. since 2014. In the course of just one legislature, ex-post evaluation has encountered a true institutionalisation and become a well-established practice: 65 such implementation reports have been initiated between 2014 and 2019 – almost two and half times as many as during the previous 2009–2014 term. The instrument was considerably reinforced in 2016, when the rules governing its use were reformed.

The EP's standing committees select the files to be evaluated according to their political priorities. However, the decision to draw up an implementation report requires a broad political backing across party lines. The report is then prepared in committee and subsequently presented to plenary for debate and vote. Once voted, the adopted resolution constitutes Parliament's formal view and therefore becomes a visible political message. Typically, the resolution addresses the observed shortcomings and calls on the executive (mostly the Commission; and to a lesser extent the EU Member States) to remedy the issues, either by better implementing the legal act or, if need be, by revising the act in question. According to the rules in place, the Commission is required to respond to Parliament within three months, detailing its actions or plans for a follow-up, or duly justifying a lack of action.[14]

While preparing such an implementation report, the committee is entitled to different means of support, which facilitate establishment of the fact base. One of these support tools is the background study ('European Implementation Assessment', or EIA) drawn up by the EP's Ex-post Evaluation Unit. This study is automatically triggered (by a general mandate from the EP Secretary-General, issued in 2014), and therefore does not require a specific committee request. While the committee has up to 12 months from the authorisation of the report to its vote in committee, the underpinning study needs to be available at an earlier stage if it is to inform the political debate. Typically, it is sent to the committee before the first exchange of views, or at the latest for the consideration of the committee's draft report. Due to its interlinkage with the committee report, this study usually receives high visibility within the EP.

As noted above, the EP's evaluation system combines the advantages of both, formal and informal scrutiny. Through its design, it contributes to evidence-based policy-making in the EP. Nevertheless, it is a time-consuming and resource-intensive undertaking, even more so as the evaluation is conducted in two simultaneous processes, one at the level of committee and the other at the research service level. However, it cannot be stressed enough that committees and Members are free to decide whether to use the study's findings or not, as the upstream study is simply a technical and non-binding resource for taking a political decision.

Other 'ex-post evaluations'

In addition, EP committees may also resort to the in-house research service for evaluations conducted outside the framework of implementation reports. EPRS has the discretion whether or not to satisfy such requests, depending on their scope as well as the resources and expertise available in-house. This category of studies, termed 'other ex-post evaluation', is subject to the same strict quality process as EIAs. As with EIAs, these evaluations are in principle and as much as possible, drawn-up in-house. However, in duly justified cases, they can also be commissioned from external experts.[15]

Requests for 'other' ex-post evaluations' increasingly come from EP temporary committees (committees of inquiry or special committees), but they may also originate from a standing committee in cases where the committee does not wish to engage in an implementation report, for whatever reason.

Given that 'other ex-post evaluations' are an informal type of evaluation (see Chapter 2.2), they are by nature a softer evaluation tool than the standard evaluation system described above (Chapter 2.3.). However, practice shows that supporting studies undertaken for temporary committees are roughly on a par with EIAs in terms of influence and visibility, as temporary committees also draw up a formal report and conclude their mandate with a resolution adopted in plenary. Moreover, their work often attracts substantial media attention, since special committees typically tackle highly topical issues such as pesticides, tax evasion, etc.

The purpose of European Parliament ex-post evaluations

Ex-post evaluation is an essential element of the European Parliament's oversight function. Parliament assesses, by means of evaluations, the transposition of EU an act by the Member States, its implementation and enforcement. In particular, it examines the impact and effect of legislation after enactment, with a focus on whether an act remains fit for purpose, years after it has entered into force. The purpose of implementation reports is defined as being to inform Parliament about an act's state of implementation, 'so as to allow the plenary to draw conclusions and to make recommendations for concrete actions to be taken'.[16]

From a methodological point of view, both the European Commission and the European Parliament ground their evaluation work on the EU's Better Regulation guidelines and toolbox, even if the EP does so less strictly and comprehensively. They both assess legislation, international agreements, policies and programmes against a standard set of criteria, including effectiveness, efficiency, continued relevance, coherence and EU added value. The EP's evaluations take any existing Commission evaluations and monitoring/information reports into account. The underlying studies also gather and analyse the views of the various stakeholders and pay great attention to academic research.

As indicated before, and contrary to the European Commission practice, the EP does not systematically review the stock of EU legislation but performs evaluation on an ad hoc basis. Trigger points for committees include public information about implementation shortcomings; input from stakeholders; input from citizens, e.g. through petitions; unsatisfactory answers to parliamentary questions; review clauses; or simply a lack of Commission action in carrying out an evaluation or initiating the revision process of an act that is deemed faulty.[17] In this respect, the main motivation for a parliamentary committee to engage in a retrospective assessment is holding the executive accountable. Indeed, accountability is in general one of the main functions of parliamentary evaluation.

However, experience shows that evaluation in the EP context also serves other purposes, notably transparency, policy learning and agenda-setting. Evaluation promotes transparency, as it examines how a law or a policy in general terms has performed in comparison with its intended objectives (impact assessments being very useful to verify this), thereby highlighting the available evidence and causalities. It addresses shortcomings in the implementation, identifies data gaps and makes recommendations on how to mitigate the observed issues. With regard to transparency, public debate and the publication of results are also important aspects. The EP resolution, the committee report and the upstream research study are retrievable on Parliament's public website. In addition, the resolution is published in the EU's Official Journal, while the study is made accessible via Parliament's public register of documents.

Furthermore, evaluation generates policy learning. This is of general interest for the EP – as co-legislator – and of even greater relevance with regard to spending programmes and policy strategies, where the EP has a say on whether to continue, adjust or terminate an initiative. In figures, 25 per cent of all EIAs carried out between 2015 and 2019 fall under this category. Policy learning can benefit topically related initiatives as well as the revision of existing legislation/programmes. In the latter case, policy learning leads to agenda-setting in the sense that evaluation findings may kick start the process of amending existing legislation. In practical terms, this equals a reset of the legislative cycle (or policy cycle).

However, unlike national parliaments, the European Parliament itself cannot start the formal revision process to amend existing legislation, since under the EU Treaties, legislative initiative is the prerogative of the European Commission. In this domain, the role of the EP is restricted to urging the Commission to take the necessary steps by means of a resolution following a legislative own-initiative report. If the Commission engages in revising an act – prompted by its own evaluation, or by an evaluation of the European Parliament or any other trigger – the legislative cycle begins its second round.

The influence of European Parliament evaluations on the policy cycle

With the eighth legislative term of the European Parliament just ended, the available data set of one complete term allows us to draw some preliminary conclusions on what has been achieved through the institutionalisation of Parliament's evaluation. This chapter first sums up Parliament's evaluation output since 2014. It then tries to shed light on the relationship between the parliamentary report on the one hand, and the research service's underpinning study on the other, that is to say how receptive committees are to using the evaluation studies. Finally, it seeks to establish whether evaluation had any tangible influence on the EU's policy cycle work.

The European Parliament's evaluation output 2014–2019

On average, the EP produces 15–20 evaluations per year (implementation reports and 'other ex-post evaluations' together). With regard to the evaluation work of the European Parliamentary Research Service during the 2014–2019 period, it completed 47 EIAs and 15 'other ex-post evaluations' for standing and temporary committees. Roughly half of these 'other requests' were conducted for temporary committees.

Parliament's broadened interest in the entire policy cycle prompted a shift in committees' attitude towards evaluation. This is a direct effect of the EU's Better Regulation agenda, which genuinely stresses the importance of evaluation for EU policy making. In this regard, Commission Vice-President Frans Timmermans (with Better Regulation, inter alia, in his portfolio) stressed the value of evaluation for EU policy-making as early as 2014. He stated that

> [w]hile the natural tendency of politicians is to focus on new initiatives, we must devote at least as much attention to reviewing existing laws and identifying what can be improved or simplified. We must be honest about what works and what doesn't.[18]

EP committees appear generally to have heeded the Commissioner's call. In the previous legislative term, two thirds of standing committees had engaged in tabling at least one implementation report. A few committees are particularly proactive in evaluation, such as the committees on Employment and Social Affairs (eight files to date); Environment, Public Health and Food Safety (six); Constitutional Affairs (five); Legal Affairs (five); Culture and Education (five); and the Committee on International Trade (five).

The interlinkage between the implementation report and the EPRS study

Drawing on Chapter 2.3., the following paragraphs describe the interlinkage between the implementation report and the supporting upstream study in more detail, in particular the ways in which the study informs the Parliament's political work.

As soon as a standing committee is granted authorisation to draw up an implementation report, the EPRS Ex-Post Evaluation Unit automatically embarks on the supporting study. The scope of this study is defined in close cooperation with the competent committee secretariat and the Member in charge of the file (the 'rapporteur'), to ensure its topical pertinence. However, the subsequent drafting is an independent process, outside the rapporteur's sphere of influence. EIAs are subject to high quality standards and they are strictly impartial. When carried out in-house, they are usually based on desk research, taking all available open-source evidence into account. In addition, for some studies, data gaps are mitigated through the collection of primary data, obtained through stakeholder consultation and/or interviews. In principle, EPRS studies are drafted by policy analysts in-house; however, when necessary (mainly because of a need for large consultations or technical or scientific analysis) and under certain conditions, in-house research may be complemented by external expertise, which is contracted through public procurement procedures, according to EU financial regulations.

In all cases, the result of the research is a comprehensive, yet easy to read, account of the implementation of the policy or the given piece of EU legislation. By its nature, particular emphasis is placed on critical issues. In the endeavour of being able to effectively inform the political debate (and subsequently the implementation report), the study needs to be made available at an early stage of the process. This time constraint often poses a challenge, in respect of the level of comprehensiveness and overall quality standards to which EPRS background studies are subject.

Effectively, in almost three quarters of cases (44 out of 62), committees invited EPRS to present the key findings either in a regular committee meeting or in the framework of a public hearing. Typically, this happens at the stage of the first exchange of views on the file or immediately before the first discussion of the rapporteur's draft (political) report. The presentation of EPRS' evaluation study is usually well received in committee. For example, when the key findings of the study examining the EU legal framework for 'Food contact materials' were presented, the rapporteur acknowledged that 'many of the conclusions the study reached are the conclusions which [she had] put into [her draft] report'.[19]

However, as stressed above, the EP committee is in no way bound to take the findings into account in its report. As Parliament is a political place and as such driven by a political agenda and interests, it is certainly conceivable that the findings of the EPRS study differ, for example, from the rapporteur's agenda. However, even in such cases, the study findings may still serve to inform the debate and in particular the amendment process where any Member, can intervene. The 2011 'Niebler report' creating the EP impact assessment capacity defined the relationship between political decision-making and research support as follows: 'Impact assessment is in no way a substitute for political debate and the legislator's decision-making process but merely serves to help the technical preparation of a political decision'.[20] This statement applies likewise to ex-post evaluation.

Having these limitations in mind, the extent to which the committees have nonetheless taken up the findings of EPRS studies is quite striking. In almost 90 per cent of cases the implementation report explicitly acknowledges or at least references the EIA as providing input, most of the time in the report's explanatory statement or in the motion for resolution. In some instances, the study is even referred to as the 'basis' or 'main source of information',[21] with substantial arguments drawing on the EIA. And occasionally, opinion-giving committees also quote or cite the study and/or some of its findings.

Similarly, with regard to Parliament's resolutions on implementation reports, data show that it is rather common that the adopted text acknowledges the upstream EIA (33 out of 47). This acknowledgement mostly takes the form of a recital, although, in a number of instances (10) more specific reference is made. In a few cases, the resolution has even incorporated substantial parts of an EPRS study.

In conclusion, based on the available data set from the 2014–2019 legislative term, it appears that EPRS supporting studies are indeed widely used by committees for their political work and contribute as such to evidence-based policy-making within the EP.

The European Parliament adheres to the principle of utmost transparency. In this respect, the committee report, the adopted resolution and the supporting ERPS study are published. This frequently resonates in the reception of EP work not only within the EP and other EU institutions, but also with the broader public (e.g. media, academia, interest groups, and sometimes the national parliaments of EU Member States[22]). This is particularly true for the work of temporary committees, which often attract strong media attention. Typically, EPRS studies carried out in the framework of a temporary committee also receive more media coverage and public attention overall than regular EIAs. Similar to EIAs, the report of a temporary committee and/or the adopted resolution usually includes detailed references to the underlying EPRS study. Likewise, it often makes good use of the findings contained in the study, as could be observed with the temporary committees on Terrorism (2017/18), on the Inquiry into Money Laundering, Tax Avoidance and Tax Evasion ('Panama committee', 2016/17) and, most recently, the Special Committee on Financial Crimes, Tax Evasion and Tax Avoidance ('TAX3', 2018/19).

Influencing the policy cycle beyond the European Parliament: first evidence

First evidence suggests that the European Parliament's evaluations have in some cases, also informed the European Commission's policy-cycle work. The number of files concerned is still relatively small however, given that follow-up in the policy cycle may be a matter of years rather than short-term, the few cases are indeed an encouraging indicator with regard to the value Parliament's own evaluations add to EU policy-making. In this respect, some Commission initiatives cite the EP resolution as provider of impetus for reviewing or revising EU legislation.

In three cases to date, the Commission has explicitly stated it had taken Parliament's ex-post assessments, together with the related resolutions, into consideration for the formulation of amending legislative proposals:

- European Citizens' Initiative, COM(2017) 482;[23]
- Discontinuing seasonal changes of time, COM(2018) 639;
- Cross-border mergers and divisions, COM(2018) 241.

The latter example will be discussed in detail below (case study 1), followed by a discussion of the EPRS study on 'Golden visas' (case study 2), a paper drafted upon the request of a special committee. This study eventually informed a pre-legislative Commission communication on a topic not yet regulated at EU level.

Furthermore, a number of the Commission's ex-ante impact assessments accompanying legislative proposals to amend existing directives or regulations, include references to Parliament's resolutions and EIAs. Similarly, with regard to the Commission's retrospective review work, EP resolutions and the linked EIA appear to have informed a certain number of Commission evaluations and fitness checks, as well as studies drawn up by external contractors. Finally, in one case, the EP resolution has, together with the linked EIA, given impetus to a fully-fledged Commission evaluation.[24]

The above-mentioned cases demonstrate that the European Parliament's evaluation system has not only the theoretical potential to directly influence the Commission's legislative policy-cycle work, but it was, in a number of actual cases, even quite successful in that respect. Based on the available data from the 2014–2019 legislative term to date, EP's evaluations have left 'fingerprints' on the Commission's work in roughly 20 cases. This figure may rise as the files advance in the policy cycle.

Case studies

Two case studies can be used to demonstrate that evidence-based analysis provided through EPRS work has actually contributed to policy-making by both Parliament and the Commission. One relates to a 'classic' legislative procedure on the issue of cross-border mergers and divisions. The other relates to the work of a special committee of the European Parliament on the issue of citizenship and residency by investment schemes ('golden passports' and 'golden visas'). The main reason why these two examples were selected over others, potentially equally eligible ones, is the fact that the authors have first-hand insight into the cases, since they were closely involved in the parliamentary process.

Case study 1: Evaluation of the EU framework in the area of cross-border mergers and divisions

General Background

The EU has progressively adopted a framework that aims at promoting a business-friendly environment at EU level and facilitating 'corporate mobility' across the Union. This framework includes legislation that enables EU enterprises to divide or merge more easily, while introducing a degree of oversight on employment security and job sustainability.

Council Regulation 2157/2001 on the 'Societas Europaea' (SE) brought important changes to EU company law in this respect. It established a European company statute and provided, for the first time, rules for mergers between public limited liability companies from different Member States through incorporation as an SE. This regulation was then supplemented by Council Directive 2001/86/EC, which contained specific rules on the involvement of employees. The negotiations on the SE Regulation opened up the debate and paved the way for further work in the area on mergers. Consequently, Directive 2005/56/EC on cross-border mergers of limited liability companies expanded possibilities for cross-border mergers to other types of companies. Concerning cross-border divisions, the EU framework is still governed by Directive 82/891/EEC, which covers divisions at national level and therefore does not lay down any rules on how to carry out cross-border divisions.

In 2012, the European Commission launched a public consultation on the future of European company law. It showed that the majority of stakeholders would be interested in further harmonisation in the field of cross-border mergers and divisions. The European Commission subsequently adopted an action plan, aimed at initiating a new framework for the future of European company law, namely by facilitating the 'freedom of establishment of companies while enhancing transparency, legal certainty and control of their operations'.[25]

In response to the Commission's action plan, the European Parliament expressed its view on the way forward for European company law in a resolution adopted in June 2012.[26] Parliament welcomed the Commission's intention to shape future initiatives designed to simplify the business environment for companies. It also stressed the importance of ensuring appropriate protection of the interests of creditors, shareholders, members and employees.

In 2014, the European Commission launched another public consultation on cross-border mergers and divisions, which focused on two main issues: the improvement of the existing framework for cross-border mergers and a possible framework for cross-border divisions. Soon after, in October 2015, the Commission issued a summary feedback on the consultation, emphasising that many respondents expressed their support for a similar legal framework for all cross-border conversions: mergers, divisions, transfer of registered office and potentially other types of conversion.

In view of the Commission's consultation and 2015 feedback report, which covers both directives (82/891/EEC and 2005/56/EC), Parliament's Committee on Legal Affairs (JURI) decided to prepare an own-initiative implementation report on cross-border mergers and divisions.

EPRS evaluation in this context

In line with the European Parliament's procedures, the committee decision to undertake an implementation report triggered a background study by EPRS, aiming at supporting the JURI Committee in its work. The study, prepared over a period of six months with the help of an external expert, presents an evaluation of the implementation and effects of the current EU legal framework in the area of cross-border mergers and divisions. In particular, it examines the ways in which Directive 2005/56/EC was implemented, as well as the limitations of Directive 82/891/EEC with regard to cross-border divisions.

The study builds on the findings of a 2013 study commissioned by the European Commission on the application of the current framework (Bech-Brun and Lexidale, 2013). It also takes account of inputs from other EU and international institutions, especially the jurisprudence of the European Court of Justice (CJEU), and the views of academia and business stakeholders.

The scope of the EPRS study was crafted in close coordination with the JURI committee secretariat. Taking the committee's interests into account, and in accordance with the Rapporteur, it looked particularly at (1) the benefits of the current EU framework; (2) the practical obstacles and/or discrepancies; (3) the extent to which the Commission's proposal for a directive relating to certain aspects of company law[27] addressed issues and matters of concern. It should be noted that, even if the scoping of a supporting study is carried out jointly with the committee and the Member leading the file, EPRS then drafts the paper independently. Furthermore, and following Parliament's call stressed in its above-mentioned 2012 resolution, the study maintained a balance between the arguments put forward for increasing opportunities for EU businesses and companies on the one hand, and the requirement to safeguard employee, minority shareholders' and creditors' rights on the other.

The EPRS analysis acknowledged the major steps taken at EU level to promote company mobility across the EU. However, it clearly underlined important remaining difficulties and obstacles, in particular concerning the limited scope of the applicable framework, the great divergence in the national protection regimes for stakeholders (creditors, minority shareholders and employees), as well as procedural and practical obstacles.

European Parliament's key role in policy learning

The study was published in December 2016 (Reynolds & Scherrer, 2016), and presented at a meeting of the Committee on Legal Affairs (JURI) in January 2017, at an early stage of the committee's deliberations. It thus served as an important source of information for the work of the committee, as was explicitly acknowledged in the committee's implementation report and the ensuing EP resolution.[28]

Eventually, the European Commission submitted a proposal concerning cross-border conversions, mergers and divisions (COM(2018) 241) in April 2018, that aimed at promoting the freedom of establishment in the Single Market on a stable basis. In both the impact assessment accompanying the proposal and the proposal itself, multiple references are made to the EPRS study, which is cited as one of the 'main inputs'. The study was explicitly used as part of the Commission's ex-post evaluation of the existing legal framework; it notably refers back to the findings of the EPRS study regarding the deficiencies of the current regime. Moreover, in the impact assessment accompanying the legislative proposal, the Commission cites the EPRS study with regard to concerns raised for stakeholders.

This case study exemplifies how the European Parliament's evaluation work, and in particular a research study underpinning a parliamentary report, can be used as a point of reference by the Commission, when updating a particular framework. In the case of cross-border mergers and divisions, the ex-post assessment conducted by Parliament contributed to push not only for improvements to the existing legal framework in the area of company mergers, but also for the launch of new initiatives in the area of divisions. The Commission's proposal was negotiated successfully and adopted by the co-legislators in autumn 2019.[29]

Case study 2: 'Golden visas'

General background

Following successive revelations in the field of tax evasion/avoidance in the past five years (Luxleaks, the Panama Papers, Football leaks and the Paradise papers),[30] the European Parliament established a Special Committee on Financial Crimes, Tax Evasion and Tax Avoidance (TAX3) in March 2018, with a twelve-month mandate. The special committee was vested with specific powers, and one of the committee's tasks was to assess national schemes providing tax privileges. In this context, EPRS was requested to prepare a study on the Citizenship by investment (CBI) and Residency by investment (RBI) schemes (known as 'golden passports' and 'golden visas') in support of the special committee.

CBI and RBI schemes are characterised by the provision of access to residency, or even citizenship in a few cases, in exchange for specified investments. Most EU Member States have such incentives in place to attract foreign investors, though their degrees and formats vary greatly (Scherrer & Thirion, 2018). Some Member States only require active investments to obtain residency rights (for instance, they require the setting up of a business on the territory that generates employment). Others require passive investments (financial capital is infused into a private company with no requirement to manage the business on a day-to-day basis or it can require a minimum lump sum transferred to government bonds or the property sector).

This evaluation request emerged in a context where news reports and/or new criminal investigations had shed light on dubious practices and scandals surrounding CBI/RBI schemes, pointing to the vulnerabilities of these schemes and potential impacts on the integrity of the internal market.[31] Anecdotal evidence indeed showed that such schemes could be used to launder money in the EU and fuelled corruption. Allegations were also made regarding potential risks associated with tax evasion (Knobel & Heitmüller, 2018).

The acquisition of national citizenship is an exclusive competence of the EU Member States and therefore not governed by EU law, even if acquiring citizenship of one EU Member State has EU implications. Regarding long-term residency rights, the EU also has limited competences. However, the risks associated with such schemes began to come to the attention of the European Parliament and the European Commission as early as 2014.[32] Both institutions underlined that schemes granting citizenship in particular were 'not neutral' with regard to the EU as a whole. Indeed, granting citizenship in one Member State gives access to rights stemming from EU citizenship.

EPRS work in this context

EPRS was first required to provide a risk assessment of these schemes that went beyond anecdotal evidence. A thorough analysis of the background checks on the integrity of the schemes' applicants and the due-diligence procedures in place confirmed serious shortcomings in relation to risks associated with money laundering. In relation to tax avoidance/evasion, EPRS work coincided with the preparation of an assessment by the OECD focusing on the extent to which RBI/CBI schemes were used to circumvent the Common Reporting Standards (CRS) and thus enable tax evasion. EPRS therefore relied partly on the results of the OECD public consultation (OECD, 2018), and came to conclusions similar to those stated by the OECD: while CBI/RBI schemes do not themselves offer a solution to evading reporting standards, they do enable false statements on residency and can thereby undermine due-diligence procedures. The OECD and EPRS also reached similar conclusions on the schemes posing a high-risk to the integrity of the CRS.[33]

EPRS was furthermore required to look at the economic and social impacts of such schemes. Using a broad range of data (official documentation, media reports, academic work), the study showed that at the economic level, CBI/RBI schemes can provide a positive contribution to Foreign Direct Investment (FDI) in the short term, but create macro-economic imbalances in the long term, in addition to putting pressure on the real estate sector. Most importantly, the study concluded that, from a policy perspective, the lack of available data on the costs and benefits of these schemes at Member State level and the uncertainties that they carry over the long term for the economy and society, constitute an important obstacle for the design and the conduct of long-term sustainable policies.

European Parliament role in agenda setting

The study by Scherrer & Thirion was published in October 2018, and its key findings were presented at a TAX3 Committee meeting the same month. They fed into the committee report, adopted in March 2019, as becomes apparent from the numerous references to the EPRS study included in the final report.[34] Based on the findings of the EPRS study, the TAX3 committee concluded that the potential economic benefits of CBI and RBI schemes do not offset the serious security, money laundering and tax evasion risks they present and called on Member States to phase out all existing CBI or RBI schemes as soon as possible.

The EPRS study furthermore informed a January 2019 European Commission communication on CBI/RBI schemes, especially in relation to risks associated with tax evasion.[35] In particular, attempts to measure the impact of these schemes, combined with an assessment of risks associated with tax evasion had hitherto been rarely touched upon, enabling the EPRS study to provide a clear added-value in the policy process. The EPRS study was in addition endorsed in an Opinion of the European Economic and Social Committee (EESC).[36]

Given the controversies surrounding the topic (including in relation to EU competences in this field), the European Commission took a more cautious stance than Parliament. While recognising – partly on the basis of the EPRS study – that these schemes raised legitimate concerns, the Commission announced that it would monitor the steps taken by Member States to ensure transparency and good governance in the implementation of CBI/RBI schemes. Several Member States reacted to the Commission's communication, including Malta.[37]

The importance of this Commission communication should not be underestimated. In fact, it is a key document to pave the way for specific actions on a topic not yet regulated at EU level. The Commission has now established a group of experts to further address matters of transparency, governance and security, and the services of EU Commissioner Reynders recently sent letters to Malta and Cyprus and are now analysing the responses. This was discussed at a European Parliament's LIBE Committee Meeting on 23 April 2020.

For this reason, the work conducted by the TAX3 special committee and EPRS' supporting role have been key to raising specific issues and outlining key challenges to be tackled at EU level. The findings of the EPRS study thus fed into a debate that is still ongoing.

Conclusions

EU-wide, ex-post evaluation capacities in parliaments remain rather the exception than the rule, despite a general trend of institutionalisation of evaluation. To date, only one third of national parliaments across the EU avail of structures that allow active ex-post evaluation of existing legislation. In this respect, the European Parliament's evaluation system, set up in the wake of the EU's Better Regulation agenda, deserves close attention. This system combines formal and informal scrutiny, in the sense that a political parliamentary report is supported by a technical study upstream, drawn up by Parliament's research service. The study underpins the report with facts, figures and options for action. This interlinkage appears to be thoroughly thought through and enjoys high acceptance amongst the EP committees. In the course of one legislature (2014–2019), ex-post evaluation has truly encountered an institutionalisation in the European Parliament, with over 60 completed evaluations.

Conducting evaluations has considerably strengthened the European Parliament's oversight function over the executive regarding the implementation of legislation. While traditionally, the core function of parliamentary ex-post evaluation is to hold the executive to account, the European Parliament's evaluations are now also increasingly geared towards policy learning and agenda setting. Unlike national parliaments, the European Parliament itself cannot start the formal revision process to amend existing legislation, since under the EU Treaties, legislative initiative is the prerogative of the European Commission. The role of the Parliament is restricted to calling, by means of an adopted resolution, on the Commission to take the necessary steps.

Nonetheless, data for the 2014–2019 legislative term demonstrate that some EP evaluations have been quite successful in influencing the Commission's policy-cycle work regarding the revision of existing EU legislation. There is evidence that EP evaluations: 1. have fed into Commission proposals to amend existing legislation; and 2. informed certain Commission ex-ante impact assessments and ex-post evaluations; or 3. otherwise informed or even triggered Commission action. This impact is illustrated by two detailed case studies. Overall, the fact that the European Parliament's ex-post evaluations have in a number of cases been successful in influencing or informing the Commission's policy cycle action could encourage other national parliaments to expand their own evaluation activities, from a passive to a more active role, to potentially strengthen their oversight function.

Notes

1. OECD, Recommendation of the Council on Regulatory Policy and Governance, 2012.
2. With the exception of Bulgaria, Croatia, Cyprus, Malta and Romania, all EU Member States are also members of the OECD.
3. The data is based on a survey conducted amongst all EU Member States. This report suggests that EU-wide, only six national parliaments (out of the then 28, thus just over 20 per cent) actively engage in ex-post evaluation.
4. The evaluation atlas covers 19 OECD countries, 10 of which are EU Member States. It assesses parliaments' active and passive involvement in evaluation, on basis of the following criteria: 1. Do parliaments carry out their own ex-post evaluations? 2. Do they initiate ad hoc ex-post evaluation (incl. commissioning to the executive)? 3. Do they introduce evaluation clauses into draft laws at the law-making stage?; and 4. Do they utilise ex-post evaluation results (produced by others) in the parliamentary debate? With the exception of Switzerland, all countries examined score relatively low, in particular compared with governmental evaluation.
5. This paper was written before Brexit became effective.
6. An earlier version of this paper was presented at the Expert Seminar on Legislative Impact Assessment and Post-Legislative Scrutiny, organised by the University of Hull and the Westminster Foundation for Democracy, on 26 April 2019 in London.
7. European Parliament resolution P7-TA(2011)0259 on guaranteeing independent impact assessments, 8.6.2011.

8. OJ L 123, 12.5.2016, pp. 1-14.
9. Other examples of parliaments performing 'informal' evaluations include Bulgaria, Latvia and Poland, where the parliamentary research services are, amongst other tasks, charged with conducting evaluation studies.
10. www.comitesuivilegislatif.be.
11. This is the 'Evaluation and Research Secretariat', an administrative entity attached to the Committee Services Division.
12. The legal base for Parliament's evaluations are the EP's Rules of Procedure and specific rules for implementation reports (adopted by the Conference of Committee Chairs).
13. European Parliament, Conference of Presidents decision of 12.12.2002, as amended, most recently on 7.4.2016.
14. Framework agreement on relations between the European Parliament and the European Commission, OJ L 304, 20.11.2010, para. 16.
15. The European Parliament has a dedicated budget line for commissioning external expertise.
16. European Parliament, Conference of Presidents decision of 12.12.2002, as amended, most recently on 7.4.2016, Annex 3.
17. Typically, the recitals section of the adopted resolution and the explanatory statement of the implementation report would give some indications on the factors that gave rise to the report.
18. European Commission press release IP/15/4988, Better Regulation Agenda: enhancing transparency and scrutiny for better EU law-making. 19.5.2015.
19. Presentation of the study before the Committee on Environment, Health and Food Safety, 23.5.2016.
20. European Parliament resolution P7-TA(2011)0259 on guaranteeing independent impact assessments, 8.6.2011.
21. E.g. implementation report A8-0165/2018 on the Ecodesign directive ('This was stressed repeatedly in an EPRS study which served as the basis for this implementation report.'); implementation report A8-0268/2018 on the Placing of plant products on the market ('A comprehensive study of the impact of the Regulation has never been carried out before. The EIA gathered new data and findings and is the main source of information for this implementation report.'); implementation report on the transport of animals A8-0057/2019 ('The findings are based, in particular, on two studies commissioned by Parliament's European Parliamentary Research Service.')
22. In the aforementioned EPRS survey, six national parliaments of EU Member States indicated to make use of EP evaluations – resolutions and underpinning studies likewise –, either in the context of parliaments' own evaluation work or more generally for parliamentary scrutiny of EU legislation.
23. Here the Commission proposal formally acknowledges Parliament's resolution and EPRS study as having 'provided input to the review process'. See COM (2017) 482, p. 7 and accompanying SWD(2017) 294, pp. 53-54.
24. European Commission, Evaluation roadmap, Evaluation of food contact materials, 28.11.2017. The evaluation roadmap is the first step in the preparation of a fully-fledged Commission evaluation.
25. European Commission, Communication on the Action Plan: European company law and corporate governance - a modern legal framework for more engaged shareholders and sustainable companies, COM(2012) 740.

26. European Parliament resolution P7-TA(2012)0259 on the future of European company law, 14.6.2012.
27. European Commission, Proposal for a Directive of the European Parliament and of the Council relating to certain aspects of company law (codification) of 3.12.2015, COM(2015) 616.
28. European Parliament resolution P8-TA(2017)0248 on cross-border mergers and divisions, 13.6.2017.
29. Directive (EU) 2019/2121 amending Directive (EU) 2017/1132 as regards cross-border conversions, mergers and divisions.
30. These leaks refer to a succession of financial scandal revealed by journalistic investigations since 2016.
31. See in particular: Organized Crime and Corruption Reporting Project (OCCRP), 'Gold for Visas' Project; Transparency International, Passport dealers of Europe: navigating the golden visa market, March 2018.
32. European Parliament resolution P7-TA(2014)0038 on EU citizenship for sale, 16.1.2014.
33. In November 2018, the OECD published a list of 'Potentially high-risk CBI/RBI schemes'.
34. European Parliament resolution P8-TA(2019)0240 on financial crimes, tax evasion and tax avoidance, 26.3.2019.
35. European Commission, Investor Citizenship and Residence Schemes in the European Union, COM(2019) 12.
36. European Economic and Social Committee, SOC/618-EESC-2019, October 2019.
37. Malta Residency Visa Agency, Press release: Reaction to the report from the Commission regarding investor citizenship and residence schemes in the EU, 23 January 2019.

Disclosure statement

No potential conflict of interest was reported by the author(s).

ORCID

Irmgard Anglmayer http://orcid.org/0000-0001-6401-3546

References

Anglmayer, I. (2020). *Better Regulation practices in national parliaments*. European Parliament, EPRS. https://www.europarl.europa.eu/thinktank/en/document.html?reference=EPRS_STU(2020)642835

Auel, K. (2017). Quality of EU legislation – the role of national parliaments. In A. De Feo, & B. Laffan (Eds.), *Scrutiny of EU policies* (pp. 53–63). European University Institute.

Bech-Bruun and Lexidale. (2013). *Study on the application of the cross-border mergers directive*. Study for the Directorate General for the Internal Market and Services. European Commission.

Caygill, T. (2019). A tale of two houses? Post-legislative scrutiny in the UK Parliament. *European Journal of Law Reform*, 21(2), 5–19. https://doi.org/10.5553/EJLR/138723702019021002002

Corbett, R., Jacobs, F., & Neville, D. (2016). *The European Parliament* (9th ed.). John Harper.

Dahler-Larsen, P. (2007). Evaluation after disenchantment? Five issues shaping the role of evaluation in society. In I. F. Shaw, J. C. Greene, & M. M. Mark (Eds.), *The SAGE handbook of evaluation* (pp. 141–160). SAGE Publications.

Griglio, E. (2019). Post-Legislative Scrutiny as a form of executive oversight: Tools and practices in Europe. *European Journal of Law Reform*, 21(2), 36–54. https://doi.org/10.5553/EJLR/138723702019021002004

Jacob, S., Speer, S., & Furubo, J.-E. (2015). The institutionalization of evaluation matters: Updating the international atlas of evaluation 10 years later. *Evaluation*, 21(1), 6–31. https://doi.org/10.1177/1356389014564248

Knobel, A., & Heitmüller, F. (2018). Citizenship and residency by investment schemes: Potential to avoid the Common Reporting Standard for automatic exchange of information. Available at SSRN: https://ssrn.com/abstract=3144444 or http://dx.doi.org/10.2139/ssrn.3144444

Leeuw, F. (2009). Evaluation: A booming business but is it adding value? *Evaluation Journal of Australasia*, 9(1), 3–9. https://doi.org/10.1177/1035719X0900900102

OECD. (2018). *Consultation document: Preventing abuse of residence by investment schemes to circumvent the CRS, 19 February 2018-19 March 2018*.

OECD. (2019). *Better regulation practices across the European Union*.

Reynolds, S., & Scherrer, A. (Eds.). (2016). *Ex-post analysis of the EU framework in the area of cross-border mergers and divisions*. European Parliament, EPRS. https://www.europarl.europa.eu/RegData/etudes/STUD/2016/593796/EPRS_STU(2016)593796_EN.pdf

Rufas Quintana, J. L., & Anglmayer, I. (2019). Retrospective policy evaluation at the European Parliament. *European Journal of Law Reform*, 21(2), 118–127. https://doi.org/10.5553/EJLR/138723702019021002013

Scherrer, A., & Thirion, E. (2018). *Citizenship by Investment (CBI) and Residency by Investment (RBI) schemes in the EU*. European Parliament, EPRS. https://www.europarl.europa.eu/RegData/etudes/STUD/2018/627128/EPRS_STU(2018)627128_EN.pdf

Post-Legislative Scrutiny in Europe: how the oversight on implementation of legislation by parliaments in Europe is getting stronger

Franklin De Vrieze

ABSTRACT
This article analyses parliamentary practices in conducting Post-Legislative Scrutiny (PLS) in Germany, Italy, France, Sweden, Switzerland and the United Kingdom against four categories of parliamentary approach in PLS. Parliaments as passive scrutinisers have few parliamentary structures, capacity and procedures for PLS and no parliamentary PLS reports. Parliaments as informal scrutinisers have few parliamentary structures and procedures but are stronger in terms of own parliamentary outputs on PLS. Parliaments as formal scrutinisers have more developed structures and procedures on PLS but remain weak in terms of outputs and follow up. Parliaments as independent scrutinisers are strong in terms of structures and procedures as well as in terms of reports and follow up. The case-studies indicate that the federal parliament of Germany is a passive scrutiniser in PLS, the parliament of Italy an informal scrutiniser, the parliaments of Sweden and France formal scrutinisers, and the UK Westminster and Swiss parliaments independent scrutinisers.

Introduction

One of the roles of parliament is to create laws that meet the needs of the country's citizens. However, it is also a parliament's role to evaluate whether the laws it has passed achieve their intended outcome(s), which is Post-Legislative Scrutiny (PLS). The act of carrying out PLS can therefore be justified as a stand-alone activity that enables a parliament to self-monitor and evaluate, as well as reflect on the merits of its own democratic output and internal technical ability.

There are two types of PLS. PLS can refer to a narrower evaluation of how a piece of legislation has been enacted and is working in practice. This type of PLS is more focused and a more purely legal and technical review. PLS can also refer to a broader review, the purpose of which is to evaluate whether and to what extent a piece of legislation has achieved its intended purpose and what is its impact.

In consequence, the act of PLS holds two distinct functions: firstly, a monitoring function, as the application of legislation and especially the adoption of the necessary secondary legislation is assessed by parliament at identified moments, and secondly an evaluation function, as parliaments seek to ensure the normative aims of policies are reflected in the results and effects of legislation. When analysing parliamentary practices in conducting PLS in different countries, both dimensions of PLS are covered in the review.

Categorisation of parliaments regarding Post-Legislative Scrutiny

Parliaments conduct Post-Legislative Scrutiny (PLS) according to different approaches. To explain how PLS progresses in parliament, this article offers a new categorisation and applies it to different parliaments in Europe. The categorisation has been designed considering the legal basis for PLS and functional variables affecting PLS.

The legal basis for PLS can be established in different ways. In a limited number of cases, PLS as a main task for parliament is based directly in the Constitution, such as in France, Sweden and Switzerland. In most cases, PLS by parliament finds a legal basis in the oversight role of parliament and its Rules of Procedure, or in review clauses and sunset clauses in pieces of legislation.

Apart from the legal basis, several functional variables shape parliament's approach in conducting PLS (Griglio & Lupo, 2019).

The first variable affects the parliament's internal organisation regarding PLS, i.e. the identification of the relevant (internal or external) units responsible for the preliminary fact-finding and analytical activity whose aim is to evaluate the effects of implementing a single piece of legislation or a selected public policy based on one or more laws. This variable shows two options. One consists of engaging external independent institutions or agencies with specific knowledge and experience in the field of policy evaluation and impact assessment (for instance, in Germany). The alternative is establishing new administrative units in parliaments in order to develop an autonomous expertise on legislative impact assessments (for instance, in Italy and Switzerland).

The second variable draws on the selection of relevant pieces of legislation and/or policies to be scrutinised, raising several options (De Vrieze, 2017, p. 12). The object of PLS can be a single piece of legislation or all legislation relevant to a selected policy. The former hypothesis usually occurs when a review or sunset clause is set in the legislative act, tasking parliament to verify that the act is correctly implemented and that expected outcomes are achieved. The latter hypothesis is locating the object of PLS in the implementation of a selected policy through different acts. This approach is more consistent with the better regulation standards promoted by the OECD and the EU (Jancic, 2019).

The third variable identifies the scope of PLS as a purely legal dimension or also comprising instances of impact assessment. In the first instance, the review only covers the monitoring of law enactment. Its aim is to check whether the implied regulations or administrative instructions have been approved, whether all the legal provisions have been brought into force, and what judicial interpretations are provided by the courts. In the second instance, parliament's scrutiny comprises forms of ex-post policy evaluation and impact assessment.

The fourth variable affects the outcomes of PLS, including its contribution to legislative decision-making and its impact on the relationship between parliament and government. PLS unfolds through two different types of parliamentary tools: the fact-finding tools, aiming at seeking information, explanation and policy positions from the government, and the oversight tools directed at holding the government to account for the outcomes produced.

Considering the legal basis and the mentioned functional variables, we have developed a categorisation consisting of four parliamentary approaches to PLS, enabling us to analyse the functioning of selected national parliaments in Europe regarding their performance in PLS.

In developing our categorisation, we reviewed the framework of Dr. Griglio (2019), which identified three main parliamentary approaches to PLS: parliaments as passive, informal and formal scrutinisers. We have finetuned this framework and designed four categories of parliamentary approaches to PLS: passive, informal, formal and independent scrutinisers. These four categories are proposed because they relate to the two main axes of analysis: the extent of parliamentary procedures and structures on PLS and the extent of parliamentary outputs on PLS.

Parliaments as passive scrutinisers have few parliamentary structures, capacity and procedures for PLS analysis, and few own parliamentary outputs on PLS in terms of reports and follow-up. Parliaments as informal scrutinisers still have few parliamentary structures and procedures but are stronger in terms of own parliamentary outputs on PLS. Parliaments as formal scrutinisers have more developed structures and procedures on PLS but are still weak in terms of outputs and follow up. Parliaments as independent scrutinisers are strong in terms of structures and procedures as well as in terms of outputs and follow up.

The four categories are designed according to an incremental logic of how much independence and capacity the parliament expresses in the fulfilment of this function. The categorisation in four approaches recognises the complexity of parliamentary institutionalisation in the area of PLS.

Table 1. Overview table of the categorisation of parliamentary approaches to PLS.

Categorisation of parliamentary approaches to PLS based on parliamentary procedures / structures on PLS and parliamentary outputs on PLS			
Organised and institutionalised parliamentary structures, capacity and procedures for PLS analysis		**Formal scrutinisers**	**Independent scrutinisers**
Few parliamentary structures, capacity and procedures for PLS analysis		**Passive scrutinisers**	**Informal scrutinisers**
Parliamentary Procedures / Structures ⟍ ⟍ Parliamentary Outputs on PLS		Little own parliamentary outputs on PLS in terms of own reports and follow-up	More parliamentary outputs on PLS in terms of own parliamentary assessment reports, 'procedimentalisation' of PLS reports and follow-up

The above Table 1 visualises the four categories along the two axes of analysis: the extent of parliamentary procedures and structures on PLS and the extent of parliamentary written outputs on PLS. The vertical axis refers to the parliamentary structures, from few to more structures and procedures. The horizontal axis refers to the parliamentary outputs, from little own parliamentary written outputs and follow up to more parliamentary outputs and follow up.

Describing the four categories in further depth, the following characteristics can be identified.

Passive scrutinisers

In the 'basic' approach to PLS, parliaments limit their role to the assessment of the scrutiny conducted by either governmental bodies or external agencies. This 'passive' approach to PLS implies that the parliament does not directly engage in monitoring legislative implementation and in impact assessment on its own, as it relies on reports and evaluations produced by the government or independent agencies.

Since most countries lack a strong parliamentary tradition in respect of impact assessment, scrutinising external reports is the most common way to engage in PLS. Due to the lack of parliamentary administrative capacity and procedures related to PLS, the PLS work is transparent in a limited way and not easily accessible to the public.

Informal scrutinisers

When parliaments decide to engage in a more proactive approach to PLS that goes beyond the mere assessment of the scrutiny activity of governmental bodies or external agencies, it requires assigning existing administrative parliamentary structures – such as research or evaluation units – to provide ex-post analysis of legislative implementation and impact assessment. The development of an internal scrutiny capacity offers parliaments autonomous resources in the fulfilment of the legislative scrutiny, additional to those offered by the government and other external structures.

Parliaments falling within this category are considered 'informal' scrutinisers insofar as the connection with the parliamentary procedures is non-systematic. This means that there are no identified or established criteria or triggers to select legislation for PLS review, but it is decided on an as-needed basis.

Formal scrutinisers

In this approach, the information gathering and analysis prior to PLS inquiries may not only be fulfilled by certain 'traditional' administrative structures – such as research and documentation units – but there is the possibility to establish a newly dedicated PLS unit or legislative impact department, adding strength to the scrutiny capacity of parliament. PLS is thus vested in specific parliamentary administrative departments or units assigned to conduct PLS. In this approach there are specific procedures for identifying laws for PLS, and there is often an explicit legal basis to conduct PLS.

While formal scrutinisers engage both in formal monitoring of law enactment (legal dimension) and in substantial impact assessment, these two activities are often mixed and formal PLS (legal dimension) prevails over substantial impact assessment of legislation.

There is a limited follow-up to the PLS findings, and there are few, if any, formal procedures providing for a debate or voting on the report in committee or plenary. Often, there is no explicit requirement for the government to respond to the PLS conclusions of parliament, and the follow up with the government takes shape through a dialogue process. In the approach of formal scrutinisers, the PLS reports are accessible to the public.

Independent scrutinisers

In the most 'advanced' approach, parliaments address PLS in an independent and highly institutionalised manner. There are specific administrative structures and committees assigned to conduct PLS. Based on their own criteria, triggers and priorities, parliament and its committees decide independently which laws to select for PLS. Parliament has a more proactive approach in identifying sources of analysis. The PLS work is legally grounded, covering both legal and impact assessment.

The institutionalised PLS work results in specific PLS reports. Parliament puts in place a more organised follow-up to the PLS reports, including by requesting government response. The 'procedimentalisation' of PLS reports is much stronger in independent scrutinisers, compared to formal scrutinisers. By 'procedimentalisation', we mean that PLS reports are supported by formal procedures providing a debate/voting of the report, for sure in committee, but potentially also in the plenary, thus granting maximum publicity to this activity.[1] Hence, in this category, PLS is fully transparent, the PLS reports are published online and thus accessible to the public.

Case-studies of Post-Legislative Scrutiny by parliaments in Europe

Taking on board this categorisation, the article considers six national parliaments in Europe (Germany, France, Italy, Sweden, Switzerland and the UK) with a view to analysing their approach to PLS. The parliaments of these countries have been selected based upon four criteria: 1/ there exist relevant parliamentary practices in PLS for more than one decade; 2/ there is enough written data and sources of information at hand; 3/ they constitute the national parliament of a European country; 4/ the elected national assembly is part of a bicameral parliamentary structure (except for Sweden).

In the following case-studies, we will analyse the administrative (Secretariat) and political (Committees) parliamentary structures and procedures for PLS, triggers for parliaments to engage in PLS, decision making to engage in PLS, transparency and availability to the public of the PLS work, and the required follow up by the government to the PLS reports of parliament.

Germany

Due to the federal structure of Germany, the upper House – the *Bundesrat* – is assigned by the Basic Law[2] formal rights both in the approval of regulations issued by the Federal Government or a Federal Minister and in the federal oversight of federal laws' execution by the *Länder*.

By contrast, the *Bundestag* conducts ex-post review of law enactment mostly resorting to the standard scrutiny or oversight mechanisms. Both formal (reporting duties, questioning, hearings) and informal channels (unofficial exchanges and contacts between members of parliaments and members of government or agencies) contribute to this goal. Ex-post reviews of executive rules by the Federal Parliament are thus a distinctive feature of the German system, whose practical effects are rather limited by the parliamentary structure of government. The ex-post review of executive rules is more a monitoring and evaluation (M&E) process for parliamentary work than a tool for oversight over the government.[3]

As for the broad dimension of PLS, impact assessment in Germany is primarily a responsibility of the government. Two independent bodies support the executive in performing this activity: the Federal Statistical Office and the National Regulatory Reform Council (NKR).[4] Regulatory Impact Assessment (RIA) is provided by the ministries and the NKR controls and provides comments. The Court of Auditors and the Federal Commissioner for Economic Efficiency are also involved.

The *Bundestag*'s engagement in ex-post impact assessment is therefore mostly carried out through governmental scrutiny or evaluation of ex-post assessments carried out by either the Federal Statistical Office or the NKR.[5] On the one hand, impact assessment arguments are preferably dealt with in parliamentary committees, which often engage in informal hearings of the responsible Minister. Moreover, MPs, either individually or through their parliamentary group, can address questions as well as interpellations to verify statements of government on ex-post impact assessment.

On the other hand, the *Bundestag* can resort to the NKR in its advisory capacity, based either on formal reporting duties to the *Bundestag* where provided by sunset or review clauses or on the standard rule on public hearings. Moreover, it is addressed the annual progress report on bureaucracy reduction and better regulation drafted by the Federal Government.

The strong reliance of the *Bundestag* on the ex-post activity carried out by the Federal Government and the NKR has apparently not prevented the parliamentary institution from starting an autonomous capacity in the field. In fact, three different bodies internal to the *Bundestag* have been able to develop some form of autonomous expertise in impact assessment: the Research Services, the Office of Technology Assessment (OTA)[6] and the Parliamentary Advisory Council on Sustainable Development. None of them is specifically devoted to PLS, but they each offer instrumental contributions with a rather differentiated impact on the activity of parliament. They work upon request and collect information on PLS when asked to do so by MPs. The activity of the Parliamentary Advisory Council on Sustainable Development should be carefully considered. Its opinions and impact assessment of Federal Government's sustainable policies are discussed and appraised in writing by the lead committee.

In view of the above information, the German federal parliament can be considered as being among the passive scrutinisers for PLS. The reasons are that, as there is preliminary reliance on government information on implementation and impact of legislation, there is limited ad hoc administrative parliamentary capacity for PLS activity while specific research units are assigned to contribute to PLS. The PLS review of the work of the government can be compared to the M&E process for parliamentary work rather than conducting their own parliamentary impact assessment of legislation. Still, there is a clear tendency to 'upgrade' the Bundestag work on PLS towards a more autonomous activity.

Italy

The case of Italy offers a significant example of PLS strongly rooted in the role of parliamentary administration (Piccirilli & Zuddas, 2012). Two ad hoc units have been established in each of the Houses in support for ex-post scrutiny. However, the 'administrative' approach to the legislative follow-up has different purposes, scopes and research/evaluation methodology in the lower and in the upper Houses, which results in asymmetric bicameralism.

In the lower House, the Chamber of Deputies, the Service for Parliamentary Oversight oversees evaluating the implementation of laws as well as monitoring reports requested from the government. The Service is expected to engage in a legal and narrow dimension of PLS, based on data provided by the government and by other institutions. It is tasked with formally monitoring the extent to which the government has respected its obligations in respect of implementation, as agreed during the parliamentary proceeding and set in statutory law. The outcomes of this 'administrative' scrutiny, originally included in the yearly Report on Legislation drafted by the Chamber of Deputies, are now published in the Report on Parliamentary Oversight that the House has released for the first time in 2017. These reports provide background information in order to reinforce the evaluation capacity of the House; however, they do not automatically trigger any procedural follow-up.

By contrast, in the upper House, the Senate of the Italian Republic, the 'administrative' approach to ex-post scrutiny combines both the narrow and the broad dimensions. On the one hand, the Service for the Quality of Regulations scrutinises the respect by the government for its reporting duties on impact assessment and monitors the adoption of implementing acts, as provided in statutory law. On the other hand, the efforts of the last few years to structure an autonomous impact assessment capacity covering a broader scrutiny and extended to impact assessment led in 2016 to the establishment of a dedicated unit – 'Office for Impact Assessment'. It is tasked with promoting studies, research, training programmes for the ex-ante and ex-post evaluation of public policies (Griglio & Boschi, 2019).

The Office for Impact Assessment is primarily tasked with research and documentation. Reports and documents are published on a dedicated website.[7] There is no procedural outcome associated with this documentation. The reform of the Rules of Procedure of the Senate approved in December 2017 has deliberately decided to leave it to MPs to elaborate on specific evaluation outcomes resorting to the standard scrutiny and oversight tools.

For both Houses, it remains difficult to evaluate whether and to what extent the activity of research and documentation strengthens the capacity of parliament to scrutinise the government. Parliamentary bureaucracies engage in ongoing monitoring of reporting duties of the Government in the ex-post stage. However, the procedural and political follow-up are often poor.

In view of the above information, the Italian bicameral parliament is considered as being among the informal scrutinisers for PLS. On the one hand, the development of an internal scrutiny units offers both chambers of the Italian parliament autonomous resources in the fulfilment of the legislative scrutiny, additional to those offered by the government and other external structures. On the other hand, the connection with formal parliamentary procedures is non-systematic, as there are no provisions of formal proceedings at the political level, by MPs and Senators, addressing the government on its follow-up to the PLS findings and recommendations.

Sweden

The role and competence of the Swedish Parliament in PLS are set in constitutional clauses, enacted in 2011, and which are implemented through statutory legislation and parliament's rules of procedure.

PLS in Sweden covers both formal and substantial verification of the implementation of the law and of the effects produced. It puts emphasis on the role of committees. The approach is that the committee that has dealt with a certain decision must be responsible for assessing whether and how the decision has been implemented. Beyond the access to governmental documents and reports, parliamentary committees have developed their own evaluation and research capacities, complemented by the interaction with other administrative units of the parliament and cooperation with the National Audit Office in Sweden.

The degree to which PLS scrutiny is performed by individual committees does vary a lot. Analysing PLS within the *Riksdag*, one Swedish political scientist (Premfors, 2015), identified three types of committees with regards to PLS activities, and the most active ones were only three out of 15 committees.[8] While the institutionalisation of PLS in the Swedish Riksdag is growing, it is not evenly and perhaps not yet at the level it could be.[9]

As is the case in France, in Sweden there is also a close interaction of the evaluation of public policies with ex-post budgetary control. The committees in the Riksdag can choose to perform two types of scrutiny. On the one hand they engage in thematic in-depth evaluations, carrying out sectorial studies focused either on a specific policy area or on the implementation of one selected piece of legislation or financing. On the other hand, they initiate a more or less broad ongoing follow-up and evaluation during their consideration of their part of the annual budget bill.

In terms of the outcomes of the scrutiny, PLS is carried out through a strong and continuous dialogue with the government, especially in regards to some committees' budget bill evaluation where groups of parliamentarians meet with the political leadership in individual ministries (often state secretaries) to discuss the results of the budget evaluation. In the sectorial studies, the outcomes of scrutiny in committee are documented in series of Reports (RFR-series)[10] that are available to the government.

However, the Riksdag committee reports are not submitted to the plenary for debate and decision. But they remain part of the committees' body of knowledge and they can sometimes be used in a later stage to adopt Parliamentary committees and are allowed to adopt a formal position on the evaluation of government performance; this can be expressed in draft resolutions or proposals for decision, addressed to the Riksdag's chamber. PLS in the Riksdag can thus trigger formal discussion of the outcomes of the evaluation process.

In view of the above information, the Swedish parliament is considered as being among the formal scrutinisers for PLS. Beyond the access to governmental documents and reports, parliamentary committees in the Riksdag have developed their own evaluation and research capacities, complemented by the interaction with other administrative units of the parliament and the cooperation with the National Audit Office in Sweden. The PLS work results in Committee reports which are the point of reference for follow up discussions with the government.

France

The competence of the French parliament regarding PLS is set in constitutional clauses resulting from the 2008 constitutional amendment. Art. 24 of the French constitution says that parliament *'passes laws'*, *'monitors Government action'* and *'assesses public policies'*.[11] Constitutional provisions are implemented through statutory legislation and parliamentary rules of procedure. The scrutiny covers both formal and substantial verification of the implementation of the law and of the effects produced.

Both chambers of the French parliament are characterised by committees that assume both legislative and oversight roles; hence, also PLS. The thematic or standing committee that has dealt with a certain decision is responsible for assessing whether and how the decision has been implemented. Follow-up and evaluation have thus become a natural task for parliamentary committees that can rely on multiple sources of information and documentation.

Beyond the access to governmental documents and reports, parliamentary committees have developed their own evaluation and research capacities. This is complemented by the interaction with other administrative units of the parliament[12] and the cooperation with the *Cour des comptes*[13] in France. Committees may rely on a large variety of oversight tools. French committees are particularly well suited in this regard as, beyond standard procedures (including questions and hearings), they have access to tools that specifically serve evaluation and inquiry purposes.

There is a close interaction between the evaluation of public policies and ex-post budgetary control. In the French National Assembly, each standing committee is responsible of following-up legislative acts that fall within its domain. However, according to the LOLF[14], budgetary ex-post scrutiny is vested in the Finance Committees of both Houses. For this purpose, in February 1999 the Finance Committee of the National Assembly created the so called 'Evaluation and Control Mission' (MEC)[15] whose main task is to inquiry into the implementation of sectorial public policies.

On the organisational side, the French National Assembly has complemented ex-post scrutiny in standing committees by creating ad hoc bodies specifically responsible for the evaluation of public policies. This trend has seen rises and falls in the last two decades, moving from bicameral to unicameral arrangements that currently exist only in the Lower House, the National Assembly, where the Committee for evaluation and control (CEC) delivers cross-sectional evaluations.[16] As a matter of fact, the hard core of PLS still lies in standing committees.[17]

The National Assembly has set up several mechanisms related to PLS (Assemblée Nationale, 2014, pp. 371–376). Firstly, there is the presentation before standing committees of implementation reports concerning laws which require the publication of rules of a regulatory nature. Secondly, there is the setting-up of temporary bodies (assessment and monitoring missions and commissions of inquiry) aimed at assessing the implementation of certain laws and public policies. The make-up of such missions can vary considerably. In practice, such missions are almost always made up of two MP's, including one member of the opposition. In cases where the fact-finding mission is set up by the Conference of Presidents, it includes nine members (a chair, four vice-chairs and four secretaries) to which must be added the position of rapporteur, and the position of chair or of rapporteur must automatically belong to an MP from an opposition group. The work of such fact-finding missions can last for varying periods, often several months, during which the members carry out interviews and visits and is concluded by the filing of an information report.[18] Thirdly, there is the development of more permanent structures: the MEC (an assessment and monitoring mission in charge of evaluating the results of certain public policies each year) set up within the Finance Committee of the National Assembly and the MECSS (the Assessment and Monitoring Mission for Social Security Financing Laws) set up within the Social Affairs Committee of the National Assembly and the Senate; the Commission for the Assessment and Monitoring of Public Policies (CEC), as well the specific parliamentary delegations.[19]

Regarding the procedural outcomes of the scrutiny, the yearly *Bilan* on law enforcement comprising scrutiny reports from all committees is submitted to the Conference of the Presidents, where an informal dialogue can be started with the government, represented by the Minister for Relationships with Parliament. However, this is an unofficial interaction whose focus is more on the fulfilment of formal implementing legal duties than on the evaluation of the economic, environmental and social impact of each piece of legislation.

For the French National Assembly, ex-post evaluation has led primarily to the reinforcement of fact-finding and inquiry tools, with no major procedural follow-up in the legislative-executive relationship. Findings are either used in the same way as other more 'traditional' parliamentary tools that support the interaction of the Houses of Parliament with government, or are debated in spontaneous forms, including the drafting of letters addressed to the Prime Minister or to the concerned Minister and the start of unofficial dialogues with the government on the required implementing measures.[20]

As far as the French Senate is concerned, the specific PLS function is by a '*Délégation*', a group of Senators charged with tasks of analysis and reflection. In the French Senate, the *Délégation of the Bureau*, carries out an assessment of the 'application of laws'; in other words, the extent to which government has enacted the dispositions necessary in order to put laws into application. On an annual basis, the chairperson of the *Délégation* presents a report developed through discussions with the seven parliamentary commissions and the Office of the Secretary General of the government, on the extent to which regulatory dispositions have been implemented. In the report dated 31 March 2017, covering the previous year, it was noted for example, that '*The rate of publication of enabling texts has reached approximately 90 per cent, in continual increase compared to the 80 per cent of last year and the 65 per cent of the session 2013–2014*'.[21] In the report of 31 March 2018, the chairperson noted that while the percentage of enabling measures enacted by the government had increased again, there was often a delay in government responses to parliamentary questions regarding application of laws.[22] The annual report on the implementation of the legislation is, in general, discussed with the government in a debate in the plenary chamber.[23]

The French Senate *Délégation* reports for both 2017 and 2018 make clear that their work is carried out in conjunction with the sectoral committees, as well as the secretariat of the Prime Minister's Office, which itself maintains records of legislative implementation within the responsible ministries.

In view of the above information, parliament's role in PLS in France can be considered as belonging to the category of the formal scrutinisers. Based on its own criteria and priorities, the French parliament decides which laws to select for PLS, though the formal monitoring of law enactment clearly prevails over impact assessment (as indicated in the '*Bilan*'). The institutionalised PLS work results in specific PLS reports. While the National Assembly and the Senate aim for follow-up to the findings and recommendations of the PLS reports, there is low degree of 'procedimentalisation', which means that PLS reports are rarely debated and voted on; and the interaction with the government on its follow up is mostly developed on informal grounds.

United Kingdom

The fifth parliament in this comparative analysis is the United Kingdom's Westminster Parliament, composed of the House of Commons and the House of Lords.

PLS is one of the core tasks of departmental (sectorial) select committees in the House of Commons.[24] A good portion of the Select Committee's activities involves PLS work, even if Members do not explicitly describe it this way (De Vrieze & Hasson, 2017).

In the last decade a more systematic approach has been taken by both the UK Government and UK Parliament (UK Cabinet Office, 2017). Since 2008 government departments have been required to prepare and publish memoranda on the Acts passed by Parliament, within three to five years of the Act entering the statue books (Kelly & Everett, 2013). The government departments are charged with conducting a 'preliminary assessment', intended to be a relatively 'light touch' (unless they wish to go deeper) but of sufficient depth to allow an informed judgement as to whether a fuller assessment by the relevant House of Commons Committee, or by a House of Lords ad hoc committee, is worthwhile.[25] These memoranda are presented to departmental select committees for additional scrutiny. With regards to the House of Lords, in 2012 the Liaison Committee promised to appoint at least one ad hoc committee per session to undertake PLS on a subject chosen by it.[26]

Recent research by Caygill (2019) into the Westminster system of PLS identified that there are differences in how the two Houses select legislation to receive PLS. In the House of Commons, PLS is one of the core tasks of departmental select committees and as such it is at their discretion to determine when to undertake such scrutiny on a piece of legislation. In relation to the House of Commons there are a number of reasons why a committee may decide to undertake PLS and select the legislation that it does, including representations by stakeholders or sectors of industry, receipt of the memorandum by a Department on the implementation of a specific law, or when there is a reasonably high level of interest among the Members.

The Liaison Committee in the House of Lords is more proactive when it comes to PLS, than its House of Commons equivalent, as it formally recommends which committees are set up and what topics are examined. As such, the ad hoc committees themselves are set up to undertake scrutiny into a particular Act and have no choice over the matter once it has been created. In terms of the factors that the House of Lords Liaison Committee considers, one of the key elements that it considers is whether the inquiry would make the best use of the expertise of Members of the House of Lords. Indeed, one of the unique selling points of the second chamber is that it contains many people with expertise in different sectors, as such, when conducting PLS it can be very valuable to tap into such expertise. Lord Norton thus rightly stated that 'in the House of Commons, PLS has been Committee-driven, whereas in the House of Lords it has been chamber-driven' (Norton, 2019).

Timing is also another important factor, in the sense that whether it is the right time to review the legislation. While the common expectation is that a memorandum is published three to five years after the Act has been adopted, one Clerk noted that 'there is an optimal time for PLS and that is five to ten years after it has come into force'.[27] The Cabinet Office Guidelines suggest indicates that it is open to the Department to propose to a Departmental Committee that a longer period is used for a particular Act, particularly so where there is a gap between the Act being passed and the provisions of the Act being brought into force. However, there are Acts for which a shorter timescale than three years might be appropriate.

Other criteria noted by clerks include that the Act should be a major one that has reformed the law in a fairly substantial way and to avoid anything too politically controversial. This is because the focus of PLS is more on the Act itself rather than looking at the underlying politics of the Act. Lord Norton's view is that

> in the House of Lords, the process of selection has been more self-contained and pro-active, the House opting for reviews that are deemed important, timely, play to the strengths of the House, and are not overly contentious politically. Whereas the Commons will examine an Act if it knows the Government is thinking of making changes to it, the Lords prefers not to engage in work it deems already underway. The House of Lords also avoids any inquiry it thinks the Commons is likely to undertake. As such, the work of the two Houses can be viewed as complementary, rather than competing with, or duplicating, the work of the other. (Norton, 2019)

Research by Caygill (2017) has highlighted the differences between the two Houses of Parliament regarding the output of their recommendations. In terms of the average number of PLS recommendations produced by each House for the sample of PLS reports analysed, the House of Lords on average produces 41 per report and the Commons, 19 per report. This is a reflection on the amount of time that the House of Lords can spend on each inquiry.

In terms of follow up to the PLS reports, the research showed that there were similarities between the two Houses on the basis that their follow up leaves a lot to be desired. If committees in the House of Commons do follow up, then they often use convenient methods, such as written correspondence or annual oral evidence sessions, rather than undertaking a follow up inquiry. This makes sense due to the time and resource pressures on House of Commons committees. This is different to the House of Lords; the challenges ad hoc committees face there are procedural as the committee is dissolved after the publication of its report. While the Lords Liaison Committee does provide the only follow up likely in the Lords, it is limited to written follow up.

In view of the above information, the role of the UK Westminster Parliament in PLS can be considered as belonging to the category of the independent scrutinisers. While the House of Commons Select Committees and the House of Lords special PLS committees always consider the initial government memorandum regarding the law under review, the Committees have their established procedures and resources for gathering information and conducting PLS. The institutionalised PLS work, which includes both legal and impact assessment, results in specific PLS reports. The UK government is required to provide a written response to the findings and recommendations within two months of publication of the report. While these features justify for the UK Westminster Parliament to be considered an independent scrutinizer, it is also recognised that Switzerland's process is even more formalised than the UK's.

Switzerland

Switzerland is a front-runner in legislative and policy evaluation. Many actors in Switzerland are involved. Federal government departments are responsible for carrying out evaluations based on an annual evaluation strategy considering the priority areas determined by the Federal Council, which is the federal government (Bussmann, 2008). The Federal Office of Justice is the body responsible for developing methodological principles related to law drafting, assisting in their application as well as being involved in legislative evaluation (Horber & Baud-Lavigne, 2019). In the area of evaluation, it collaborates with the Swiss Evaluation Society (SEVAL). An evaluation network also exists within the federal administration (De Vrieze & Hasson, 2017).

Switzerland was the first country to introduce an evaluation clause at the constitutional level: art.170 of the Swiss Constitution of 18 April 1999 calling the bi-cameral Federal Assembly to ensure that federal measures are evaluated regarding their effectiveness. The legal basis for PLS was further expanded by the law on the functioning of Federal Parliament (2003):

> The organs of the Federal Assembly designated by law shall ensure that the measures taken by the Confederation are evaluated as to their effectiveness.

To this end, they may: 1. Request the Federal Council to have impact assessments carried out; 2. Examine the impact assessments carried out on the instructions of the Federal Council; 3. Instruct impact assessments to be carried out themselves (art. 27).

Two parliamentary committees – the Control Committees – one for each of the two chambers of parliament, play a central role in evaluation.[28] To assist these two Oversight Committees, in 1991, the Federal Assembly set up the *Parliamentary Control of the Administration* (PCA), a specialised service that carries out evaluations on behalf of the Parliament.[29]

As a Unit within the Parliamentary Service, the legal bases of the PCA are set out in the Parliament Act and the Parliamentary Administration Ordinance. They provide the PCA with substantial rights to information:

(a) the PCA deals directly with all federal authorities, public agencies and other bodies entrusted with tasks by the Confederation and may request from them all relevant documentation and information,
(b) the principle of professional confidentiality does not restrict the authorities' obligation to provide information,
(c) the PCA may call on the services of experts outside the federal administration, who are therefore granted the necessary rights. The independence of the Unit is also mentioned in the Ordinance. The recruitment and appointment of the head and staff of the Unit happens according to the parliamentary service recruitment rules.

The Unit was created at a time when there was public perception that the Ministries did not share information as required. Parliament wanted to strengthen its oversight role.

The evaluations are developed based upon a mandate received by the Oversight Committees. Since 2003 the other parliamentary committees can also ask the PCA for evaluations. In practice it is almost exclusively the Control Committees that used the expertise of the PCA.[30] The Unit cannot decide to conduct evaluations on its own. The Unit makes suggestions, but it is for Committees to decide what is followed-up on. The Unit has a list of criteria that must be fulfilled for it to suggest an evaluation. Main criteria are the presence of potential problems in the policy field of interest and a gap in the availability of information or analysis. Another criterion is the likelihood that the legal basis of the policy under investigation will not be changed in the next two or three years and, therefore, that the outcome of the research remains relevant when the study has been completed.

The Committees decide based on short descriptions of the topics that fulfil the criteria. Once the Committees decide which topics will be researched, the Unit drafts a project outline of the research, including its methodology and options (on content).[31]

There is a close link between policy evaluation and legislative evaluation. The Unit usually starts with the evaluation of a policy area, which might be affected by various laws, and verifies the legal basis of what the ministries are doing and whether the laws indeed have the desired effects.

The follow-up to evaluation reports are not conducted by the Unit itself. The Unit presents the findings to the Committee, and the Committee decides on the recommendations it can deduct from the research. The PCA does not interfere in the process of compiling the recommendations, since it is more of a political process. This contributes to the independence of the Unit. These recommendations of the Committees have usually been transformed into governmental ordinances, or into acts at the ministerial level, aimed at modifying the implementation process toward the direction suggested by parliamentary Committees (Griglio & Lupo, 2019).

The control committees of both Chambers intervene in the evaluation process in three subsequent stages. First, they order the PCA to carry out evaluations, giving notice to the Federal Council. Second, they provide a political follow-up to the PCA's evaluations by drawing relevant conclusions and formulating recommendations to the Federal Council. Third, the Control committees can also draft a motion, based on the PCA's evaluations, in order to submit an amendment request to the Federal Council. The submission of these recommendations and requests starts a dialogue between the Federal Council and the relevant control committee. After two years, control committees usually start a post-evaluation follow-up to assess the implementation of the recommendations submitted to the Federal Council.

In view of the above information, the role of the Swiss federal parliament in PLS can be considered as belonging to the category of the independent scrutinisers. The institutionalised way of conducting PLS relies on specific administrative structures assigned to conduct PLS. Based on their own criteria and priorities, the Swiss parliament and its committees decide independently which laws or policy fields to select for PLS. The parliament has a proactive approach to identifying sources of analysis. The PLS work is legally grounded, in the constitution and in law, covering both legal and impact assessments of legislation. The institutionalised PLS work results in specific PLS reports. Parliament puts in place a more organised follow-up to the PLS reports, with Committees drafting recommendations in most cases. The recommendations are addressed to the Federal Council. Their transformation into governmental ordinances, or in acts at the ministerial level, ensures substantial results of the PLS work by the federal parliament of Switzerland.

Conclusion

The case-studies demonstrate how PLS has been positively included in daily parliamentary practices, in different ways. Whereas PLS is not among the traditional functions of representative assemblies, in the last decade the attempts to situate PLS among parliamentary tasks have significantly increased.

The case-studies highlighted that parliaments' involvement in this sphere might be supported either by 'administrative' strategies, such as the strengthening of the documentation and evaluation capacity of parliaments or by 'political' strategies focused on the reinforcement of parliaments' influence on governments in the ex post stage.

Four models have subsequently been identified to describe the main approaches of parliaments regarding these mechanisms: passive, informal, formal and independent scrutinisers. Based on the analysis of the case-studies, we have concluded that the federal parliament of Germany can be considered a passive scrutiniser, the parliament of Italy can be considered an informal scrutiniser, the parliaments of Sweden and France can be considered formal scrutinisers, and the parliaments of the UK and Switzerland can be considered independent scrutinisers in PLS.

As PLS is a broad concept, the case-studies demonstrate that it might mean slightly different things to different parliaments and stakeholders. In a narrow interpretation, PLS looks at the enactment of the law, whether the legal provisions of the law have been brought into force, how courts have interpreted the law and how legal practitioners and citizens have used the law. In a broader sense, PLS looks at the impact of legislation; whether the intended policy objectives of the law have been met, as well as the degree of its efficiency. The article thus highlighted how different parliaments put more emphasis on one or the other of the two dimensions of PLS. We therefore conclude that, to the extent that parliaments seek to carry out both dimensions, PLS facilitates continuously improvement of the law itself and policy implementation. PLS thus contributes to increased governance effectiveness and accountability.

Notes

1. Author's correspondence with Dr. Elena Griglio, Italian Senate, September 2019.
2. Art. 53 of the Constitution of the Federal Republic of Germany.
3. Author's correspondence with Jochen Gukes, Parliamentary Support Programmes Coordinator, German Bundestag, in September 2019.
4. The role of the NKR is to ensure that all government legislative proposals are based on an ex-ante regulatory assessment.
5. Ex-post legislative regulatory impact assessment is conducted in Germany in three cases: 1/ when it is so provided by the explanatory memorandum for the bill (art. 44 of the Joint Rules of procedure of the Federal Ministries); 2/ when legislative proposals overcome certain thresholds of annual compliance costs (Decision of State Secretaries 'Strategy for evaluation of new legislative proposals', in The Federal Government, Better Regulation 2012: Reducing Regulatory Burden, Cutting Red Tape, Securing Dynamic Growth, Berlin,

Federal Chancellery, 2013, p. 62); and 3/ when evaluation is provided by specific review or sunset clauses included in the legislative act (www.normenkontrollrat.bund.de).
6. The Office of Technology Assessment at the German Bundestag is an independent scientific institution created with the objective of advising the German Bundestag and its committees on matters relating to research and technology. https://www.tab-beim-bundestag.de/en/about-tab/index.html.
7. The first annual report of the Office for Impact Assessment of the Italian Senate mentioned that the Office has conducted 30 evaluations in the period 2017–2018. The report has been published at: http://www.senato.it/application/xmanager/projects/leg18/attachments/documento/files/000/029/081/A_year_of_assessment.pdf.
8. The three (then) most active committees were, according to Premfors, the Committee on Agriculture, the Committee on Culture and the Committee on Transportation.
9. Author's correspondence with Thomas Larue, Director of Secretariat, Riksdag's Research and Evaluation Secretariat, August 2019.
10. See the series 'Reports from the Riksdag', http://www.riksdagen.se/en/documents-and-laws/docs--laws/reports-from-the-riksdag/.
11. The role attributed to Parliament in post-legislative scrutiny is deeply rooted in the French tradition, but only with the constitutional reform of 2008, the role of parliament in the evaluation of public policies was definitively recognised as a constitutional obligation. Art. 24 of the French constitution says that parliament '*passes laws*', '*monitors Government action*' and '*assesses public policies*'.
12. In the case of France, the reference is to the Parliamentary Office for the Evaluation of Scientific and Technologic Options, a bicameral body established in 1983 that is responsible of assessing the impact of scientific and technologic reforms. See Assemblée Nationale, 2014.
13. See art. 47 of the French Constitution and art. 58.2. LOLF, allowing Finance committees to assign the *Cour des comptes* the task to carry out special inquiries on specific issues, to be concluded in eight months. Assemblée Nationale, 'Les enquêtes demandées à la Cour des comptes (article 58-2° de la LOLF)', 2011 (www.assemblee-nationale.fr/commissions/cfin_enquetes_Cour_comptes.asp).
14. LOLF stands for *loi organique relative aux lois de finances*, or the French budget law.
15. MEC is co-chaired by two members, one from majority and the other from opposition, and it is composed of 16 members, all belonging to the Finance committee, designed by parliamentary groups as to respect an equal representation of majority and opposition.
16. http://www2.assemblee-nationale.fr/15/commissions-permanentes/commission-des-finances/printemps-de-l-evaluation/edition-2019/(block)/55716.
17. Author's correspondence with Guillaume Renaudineau, French Senate, July 2019.
18. http://www2.assemblee-nationale.fr/documents/liste/%28type%29/rapports-application-loi/%28legis%29/15.
19. Author's correspondence with Marie Vigouroux, French National Assembly, September 2019.
20. Art. 60 LOLF calls the government to give, within two months, a formal written reply to Committee reports.
21. http://www.senat.fr/rap/r16-677/r16-6770.html.
22. https://www.senat.fr/notice-rapport/2017/r17-510-notice.html.

23. Author's correspondence with Guillaume Renaudineau, French Senate, July 2019.
24. In September 2019, the House of Commons Liaison Committee's report on the effectiveness and influence of committees has revised the core tasks of Committees and included PLS as part of a broader policy task rather than a task on its own. See House of Commons Liaison Committee, 2019. On the other hand, the Liaison Committee of the House of Lords has recently reaffirmed its commitment to PLS.
25. Author's correspondence with Mr. Crispin Poyser, UK House of Commons, July 2019.
26. House of Lords Liaison Committee. *Review of select committee activity and proposals for new committee activity,* March 2012. HL 279.
27. Tom Caygill's interview with the Clerk of the House of Lords Liaison Committee, 2018.
28. The CdG are composed of 25 members at the National Council and 13 members at the Council of States. Members are elected for a four-year term with the possibility of renewing the mandate. The composition of the Committees and the selection of the Chair and Deputy Chair depend on the strength of the parliamentary groups established within each House. As far as possible, the official languages and regions of the country are also considered.
29. http://www.parlament.ch/e/organe-mitglieder/kommissionen/parlamentarische-verwaltungskontrolle/Pages/default.aspx.
30. Author's correspondence with Felix Strebel, PCA, September 2019.
31. Author's interview with Simone Ledermann of PCA, March 2016.

Disclosure statement

No potential conflict of interest was reported by the author(s).

Note on contributor

Franklin De Vrieze is Senior Governance Adviser in the Technical Advisory Unit at the Westminster Foundation for Democracy in London.

ORCID

Franklin De Vrieze http://orcid.org/0000-0001-5054-1313

References

Assemblée Nationale. (2014). *The national assembly in the French institutions* (English translation). Paris: Assemblée Nationale Service des affaires internationales et de défense. Retrieved October 10, 2019 from http://www.assemblee-nationale.fr/connaissance/fiches_synthese/septembre2012/national-assembly.pdf

Bussmann, W. (2008). The emergence of evaluation in Switzerland. *Evaluation, 14*(4), 499–506. https://doi.org/10.1177/1356389008095491

Caygill, T. (2017). *Post-Legislative Scrutiny: What recommendations are committees making, and are they being accepted?* Retrieved October 10, 2019 from http://

blogs.lse.ac.uk/politicsandpolicy/post-legislative-scrutiny-strength-of-recommendations/

Caygill, T. (2019). A tale of two houses? Post-Legislative Scrutiny in the UK parliament. *European Journal of Law Reform*, 21(2), 5-19. https://doi.org/10.5553/EJLR/138723702019021002002

De Vrieze, F. (2017). *Post-Legislative Scrutiny: Guide for parliaments*. WFD. Retrieved October 10, 2019 from https://www.wfd.org/2018/07/23/a-guide-to-post-legislative-scrutiny/

De Vrieze, F., & Hasson, V. (2017). *Post-Legislative Scrutiny. Comparative study of practices of PLS in selected parliaments and the rationale for its place in democracy assistance*. WFD.

Griglio, E. (2019). Post-Legislative Scrutiny as a form of executive oversight: Tools and practices in Europe. *European Journal of Law Reform*, 21(2), 36-54. https://doi.org/10.5553/EJLR/138723702019021002004

Griglio, E., & Boschi, M. (2019, April 26). *How to structure Post-Legislative Scrutiny in parliament: Insights from the Italian Senate*. Paper presented at the Expert Seminar on Legislative ex post Evaluation, Legislative Impact Assessment and PLS, co-organised by the Centre for Legislative Studies of the University of Hull and by the Westminster foundation for Democracy, London.

Griglio, E., & Lupo, N. (2019, June). *Parliaments in Europe facing the challenge of Post-Legislative Scrutiny: Comparing the French, Italian and Swiss experiences*. Paper presented at the Academic Conference on Post-Legislative Scrutiny in Asia, Westminster Foundation for Democracy, Yangon.

Horber, P., & Baud-Lavigne, M. (2019). Factors contributing to the strong institutionalization of policy evaluation in Switzerland. In A. E. Ladner et al. (Ed.), *Making the state work successfully* (pp. 355-372). Palgrave Macmillan.

House of Commons Liaison Committee. (2019). *The effectiveness and influence of the select committee system* (Fourth Report of Session 2017-19). Retrieved October 10, 2019 from https://publications.parliament.uk/pa/cm201719/cmselect/cmliaisn/1860/1860.pdf

Jancic, D. (2019). Better regulation and Post-Legislative Scrutiny in the European Union. *European Journal of Law Reform*, 21(2), 55-71. https://doi.org/10.5553/EJLR/138723702019021002005

Kelly, R., & Everett, M. (2013). *Post-Legislative Scrutiny*. House of Commons Library, SN/PC/05232. Retrieved October 10, 2019 from https://researchbriefings.parliament.uk/ResearchBriefing/Summary/SN05232

Norton, P. (2019). Post-Legislative Scrutiny in the UK parliament: Adding value. *The Journal of Legislative Studies*, 25(3), 340-357. https://doi.org/10.1080/13572334.2019.1633778

Piccirilli, G., & Zuddas, P. (2012). Assisting Italian MPs in pre-legislative scrutiny: The role played by Chambers' counsellors and legislative advisors in enhancing the knowledge and skills development of Italian MPs: The assistance offered to an autonomous collection of information. *Parliamentary Affairs*, 65(3), 672-687. https://doi.org/10.1093/pa/gss023

Premfors, R. (2015). *Riksdagen utvärderar*. Förvaltningsakademin vid Södertörn högskola. Retrieved October 10, 2019 from https://www.diva-portal.org/smash/get/diva2:862410/FULLTEXT01.pdf

UK Cabinet Office. (2017). *Guide to making legislation*. Cabinet Office. Retrieved October 10, 2019 from https://www.gov.uk/government/publications/guide-to-making-legislation

How parliaments monitor sustainable development goals – a ground for application of post legislative scrutiny

Fotios Fitsilis and Franklin De Vrieze

ABSTRACT
The United Nations 2030 Agenda is a global framework for sustainable development. This article sheds light on the engagement of parliaments to control the implementation of sustainable development goals (SDGs). For this purpose, institutional and non-institutional measures from a wide range of parliaments were evaluated and a general assessment framework has been developed, leading to the determination of a set of basic types of dedicated parliamentary bodies that handle SDG related issues and the nature of their cooperation with extra-parliamentary stakeholders. In this context, the Post-Legislative Scrutiny concept, which assesses both legal and impact dimensions of the implementation of law, has been studied, in order to prove whether it constitutes a viable long-term contribution in accelerating the achievement of the SDGs. Based on examples of good practice, the article presents tangible recommendations and urges parliaments to upscale action related to improving efficiency in the achievement of the SDGs.

Introduction

Adopted in 2015, the United Nations (UN) 2030 Agenda is a global framework for sustainable development, setting 17 Sustainable Development Goals (SDGs) and 169 sub-objectives related to the most significant economic, social, environmental and governance issues worldwide. For the purpose of this article, sustainable development can be defined as:

> development that meets the needs of the present without compromising the ability of future generations to meet their own needs. (World Commission on Environment and Development, 1987, chapter 2, para. 1)

It is a rather dynamic concept, evolving through time and based on three pillars; environment, the economy and society (Robert et al., 2005, p. 12).

The 17 SDGs integrate all the pillars of sustainable development, comprising an urgent call for action by all countries (UN, 2019a). The SDGs continue the legacy of the Millennium Development Goals (MDGs), with some innovations. For instance, the number of SDGs is increased comparing with the original 8 MDGs. Additionally, the SDGs involve every country worldwide, both developing and developed, in contrast to the MDGs that referred only to developing countries (ALDA, 2016, pp. 3–4).

Compared to the MDGs, there is a new goal, Goal 16, which focuses on effective, transparent, accountable and participatory governance. In order for this to be achieved, access to justice and effective, accountable and inclusive institutions are necessary (Datta & Rabbany, 2016, p. 8604; TAP Network, 2016, p. 1). In addition, Datta and Rabbany (2016) conclude that effective, accountable and inclusive institutions including Parliaments are highly important for the implementation of all other SDGs. Clearly, there is a unique interaction between parliaments and the SDG 16. By holding public hearings, requesting clarifications directly from government and reports from plenary sessions, parliaments can turn public attention to the SDGs, encouraging accountability at all levels (SDG 16 Hub, 2019).

While the mandate for implementing the above goals and objectives is vested in the Executive of each UN member state, the parliaments are entrusted with the equally important role of debating and passing the related legislative measures, as well as supervising their implementation. Earlier studies already attempted to systematise parliamentary conduct in relation to SDGs, as well as to collect information on parliamentary involvement (Deveaux & Rodrigues, 2018). This article contributes further to this work and sheds additional light on the engagement of parliaments to control implementation of SDGs. For this, institutional and non-institutional measures from several parliaments were evaluated with the aim of mapping parliamentary involvement and to develop a general framework for the impact of parliaments in monitoring SDGs. Furthermore, the extent of involvement in relation to budgetary issues for SDG implementation has also been screened. The article represents the result of a two-year long global study on the efficiency and effectiveness of parliamentary monitoring of the SDGs (Fitsilis & Zisioglou, 2019). It constitutes the first general evaluation of the study, discusses its main findings and provides food-for-thought for further action.[1] Further contributions to follow will deal with regional aspects of parliamentary involvement.

Post-Legislative Scrutiny (PLS) constitutes a recent development in parliamentary procedures and practices aiming at strengthening parliamentary oversight on the implementation of legislation, as part of the oversight function of parliament. PLS has been developed across two main dimensions: the assessment of law enactment and the evaluation of the degree of achievement of its policy objectives. PLS can be used to assess individual pieces of legislation but it can also be applied to an entire legal framework or set of laws.

Here, PLS principles, as published by the Westminster Foundation for Democracy (WFD), are tested to ensure that they are compatible with the implementation and monitoring regime of the SDGs. A landmark case study can be found in the Indonesian Parliament, which has established solid structures, procedures, resources and practices of conducting PLS on a wide set of laws. For instance, a recent PLS on the Fisheries Act highlighted the current state of safeguarding the marine environment and addressing the challenge of fishing by foreign vessels in Indonesian waters (Trihartono et al., 2019). This article studies the intersection between parliamentary monitoring of SDGs and the application of the PLS technique.

The basic research question is therefore: what constitutes the engagement of parliaments to control the implementation of SDGs and which institutional and non-institutional measures have selected parliaments around the world taken in order to ensure their involvement? Based on the review of selected existing good practice, the article offers a series of recommendations and urges parliaments to upscale their action to support the success of SDGs, as an additional means to strengthen their own position in the institutional system. The principal goal of the study is to reveal the role of parliaments in SDG monitoring and their contribution to the successful implementation, based on a quantitative set of data made available through the mentioned global study on SDGs and parliament. In this regard, the article highlights the contribution of Post-Legislative Scrutiny as an *oversight tool* on the implementation of legislation relevant to the implementation of the SDGs. Another research question is thus: can PLS play a significant role in assisting parliaments to achieve their central oversight role?

Policy and implementation

In 2015, during the 70th Summit of the General Assembly of the United Nations, the member states convened a special summit in order to determine the developmental programme after the previous programme adopted by the UN General Assembly in 2000, which consisted of the MDGs. This special summit adopted a new Declaration, the National Agenda for Sustainable Development (Transforming Our World – the 2030 Agenda for Sustainable Development), which includes 17 universally applicable targets, i.e. the Sustainable Development Goals. The SDGs reflect a more holistic approach to global development, the survival of humanity and respect to the planet and constitutes the driver for the formulation of national policies of the member states of the United Nations and for improved international cooperation until the year 2030 (ICLEI, 2015, pp. 1–2).

As the 2018 SDGs Report indicates, progress has been made in many areas of the 2030 Agenda the previous years. For example, worldwide, the participation rate in early childhood and primary education increased to 70 per cent in 2016, from 63 per cent in 2010 (UN, 2018a, p. 6), while by 2018, 108 countries had national policies and initiatives relevant to sustainable consumption and production (UN, 2018a, p. 10). Despite this progress, there are many challenges concerning each one of the 17 SDGs. For instance, based on 2016 estimates, only 45 per cent of the world's population were effectively covered by at least one social protection cash benefit (UN, 2018a, p. 4). World hunger is on the rise again: 815 million people were undernourished in 2016, an increase of almost 40 million people since 2015 (UN, 2018a, p. 4). Earning inequalities between women and men are still pervasive. Men earned 12.5 per cent more than women in 40 out of 45 countries supplying data, while youth were three times more likely to be unemployed than adults in 2017 (UN, 2018a, p. 8).

According to a recent survey that covers all 193 UN member states, no country was identified as being on track to achieving all of the goals (Sachs et al., 2019, p. viii). In its 2018 edition (Sachs et al., 2018, pp. 2–3), in terms of how strongly the SDGs were integrated into institutions and policy among the G20 countries, which measures only whether plans are in place and not how effective they are, the survey revealed the countries with the strongest institutional support for the global goals were Brazil, Mexico, and Italy, where specific SDG strategies and co-ordination across government departments have been adopted. Interestingly, US ranked last ahead of Russia. Generally, progress in the field of SDGs has been slow. Moreover, no country in the G20 has aligned their national budget to meeting the SDGs and until 2018 only India has done a complete projection of the additional funding needed (Nelson, 2018; Sachs et al., 2018, p. 5).[2]

Oversight of SDGs

As mentioned above, SDG 16 indicates that the establishment of 'effective, accountable and inclusive institutions' is vital for the implementation of the SDGs. The final Agenda 2030 document encourages member states to conduct regular and inclusive reviews of progress at the national and subnational levels which are country-led and country-driven. Furthermore, it is stated that national parliaments as well as other institutions can also support these processes (House of Commons, 2016, p. 52). The Resolution adopted by the United Nations General Assembly on 25 September 2015 also highlights the important role of Parliaments in the implementation of the SDGs through the enactment of legislation and adoption of budgets and their role in ensuring accountability for the effective implementation of the SDGs' (see General Assembly resolution 70/1 in UN, 2015).

The 2030 Agenda reaches across many, if not all, aspects of government and parliamentary business. A parliament's constitutional responsibility to steer their country's sustainable development directly impacts SDG implementation whether it is framed this way or not (Together 2030, 2018, p. 6). Based on the 2030 Agenda, national parliaments have three main responsibilities, which are directly related to the implementation of the Agenda: they pass laws, approve budgets and hold government agencies accountable. These responsibilities constitute an integral part towards successful implementation of the 2030 Agenda (Mulholland, 2017, p. 5).

Oversight on SDGs can basically be broken down into two distinct levels. The policy level takes place in supranational organisations, such as the Inter-Parliamentary Union (IPU), the United Nations (UN), but also regional ones, such as the Economic Community of West African States (ECOWAS) and the European Union (EU). The implementation level covers the national states which are responsible for the specification and localisation of the goals. The following paragraphs shed light on the policy level at the supranational policy level, as the world study that is presented herein shows the conduct on the national level in great detail.

UN

The United Nations System has a pivotal role in supporting member states in the implementation of SDGs. Inter-agency coordination is achieved through the Executive Committee of Economic and Social Affairs Plus (ECESA Plus), which brings together 50+ UN entities and research institutes. ECESA Plus is supported by the Department of Economic and Social Affairs (UN-DESA). In addition, the Chief Executives Board (CEB) and the United Nations Sustainable Development Group (UNSDG) coordinate follow-up activities in their respective areas across the UN system (UN, 2019b).

EU

The EU has a structured approach towards implementing the 2030 Agenda. The European Commission (2016, p. 18) committed to the delivery of the Agenda and proposed a series of actions. As a consequence, the Commission set-out 10 political priorities and established a high-level multi-stakeholder platform on the implementation of SDGs. In order to monitor implementation in an EU context, Eurostat (2019) has created a dedicated website. For SDG 16, according to Eurostat, significant progress towards several EU targets seems to have been achieved.

IPU

One of the roles of IPU is to help parliaments achieve the objectives of the SDGs, by providing assistance and policy guidance to parliaments (IPU, 2018). IPU organises regional and inter-regional seminars for parliaments in order to bring attention to the SDGs and to promote cooperation at a regional level (IPU, 2018). On the other hand, at the national/local level, IPU engages with specific field missions (needs assessment missions) to parliaments to assess their capacity to integrate SDGs via dedicated legislation. In this regard, IPU's self-assessment toolkit can be useful, as it has been designed to assist legislatures to identify good practices, gaps and opportunities when integrating SDGs into their work (IPU, 2018). Finally, at the UN level, IPU organises parliamentary side events at the High-Level Political Forum (HLPF) on Sustainable Development (HLPF, 2019), which is the UN's central platform for the follow-up and review of the 2030 Agenda for Sustainable Development and SDGs (UN, 2019b).

Parliaments need to engage in the implementation and oversight of the entire SDG framework. But they also need to pay special attention to their own institutional development in line with targets 16.6 and 16.7. For example, parliaments can work with their national statistics authority to develop indicators that reflect their own priorities in support of targets 16.6 and 16.7 (IPU, 2016, p. 7). However, one should keep in mind that SDGs is neither a mandatory nor a strict framework. In addition, range, timing and depth of implementation are up to the national states to decide. This would mean that related legislation would enter the parliament gradually, one by one or in clusters. Hence, technically, SDG related legislation is not to be distinguished from 'regular' legislation. The following section presents the scientific goals of this article as well as the methodological approach.

Research goals and methodology

While a lot is known and reported on the significance and the implementation side of SDGs, little can be found about parliamentary involvement. This article aims, therefore, to shed light on the role of parliaments, their methods and approaches to oversee and control governmental actors in the exercise of SDGs related policies. Another significant motive for this work was to provide feedback to the international community, regional actors and single states on how parliaments approach the challenge of monitoring the implementation of SDGs. As scientific contributions on parliaments and SDGs are rather scarce,[3] this study offers an easily accessible and transparent dataset to the academic community and beyond, which is based on an on-going global study on parliamentary monitoring of the SDGs. The dataset is openly accessible and offered under a Creative Commons license (CC BY). The community is invited to gain access in order to reproduce the results and conduct further investigations.

The article attempts a structured response to two basic research questions:

(1) What is the involvement of parliamentary institutions in the oversight of SDGs?

Should monitoring activities by parliaments prove significant, what are the options, e.g. in terms of mechanisms or techniques to conduct such activities? Hence, the follow-up question is:

(2) Can PLS play a significant role in assisting parliaments to achieve their oversight role?

In order to tackle these issues, the mentioned dataset was evaluated to identify levels of parliamentary involvement. In a second step, the principles of PLS have been screened to prove that it can be used to sufficiently advance the capacity of legislatures to monitor the SDGs.

The dataset includes data on intra- and extra-parliamentary conduct and control of the budget related to the implementation of the SDGs, i.e. SDG budget. It contains 154 entries, which correspond to 153 UN member states, as well as Palestine, as an observer to the UN. Particular attention was paid to the sources of data to ensure the overall validity, and hence the quality, of the results. For methodological clearance, analysis was based only on written text from official sources, e.g. Voluntary National Reviews (VNRs) and policy documents, scientific literature and existing meta-studies (Power, 2012; UN, 2018b).[4]

The dataset integrates information from snapshots over different points in time, as for example VNRs of different countries were not generated and submitted altogether. Hence, it is difficult to obtain a unified picture in the present and in real time. Throughout this study several challenges were encountered that were related to the quality of textual data, such as language barriers or the use of ambiguous expressions. Also, translation of VNRs to a language of reference, here: English, can frequently be error-prone. To the knowledge of the authors, this is the first time that an effort to analyse parliamentary conduct on a global level in relation to the SDGs based on quantitative data has been attempted. Data collection ended in December 2018. A review should be conducted within a two-year frame to show progress and/or modifications in the parliamentary approach to SDG monitoring.

Analysis

The analysis evaluates the previously mentioned dataset, which has been made available through an open format to all stakeholders. Data evaluation based on transparent analysis followed a structured pattern. The classification used of UN member states is geographical but not related to the UN regional groups. Instead, a standard continental classification, with some distinct political geographical elements was used. 153 out of 193 member states of the UN, i.e. 79.3 per cent of the member states, were examined.[5] With reference to the remaining member states, at the time of drafting, no official information could be retrieved, such as VNRs or national policy documents. In this context, it must be noticed that, since no information on the remaining 20.7 per cent of the UN member states could be harvested, these 153 countries constitute the basis for the calculations.

A rather balanced representation of member states from the European (39), African (38) and Asian (41) continents has been detected, each of which contributed with roughly one fourth of the sample population. America (24) follows with relatively fewer member states, followed by Oceania (11). These proportions and their percentage points are visible in Figure 1.

Figure 2 shows the wider picture of parliamentary involvement. Overall, from 153 examined countries, it was found that 64 countries have, or will have soon, direct parliamentary involvement regarding SDGs. This number is particularly high when one considers that just a few years ago, in 2015, it was equal to zero. Europe has the highest contribution of member states (20) that are directly involved with SDGs. However, if one sees the glass half-empty, one could say that only half of the examined European countries, i.e. 20 out of 39, display parliamentary participation in the implementation and/or monitoring of SDGs. A rather surprising fact was found in Oceania's participation, i.e. two out of the 11 examined member states showed signs of parliamentary involvement. Considering that many countries in Oceania are

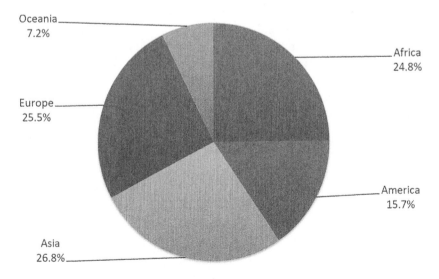

Figure 1. Examined countries per continent.

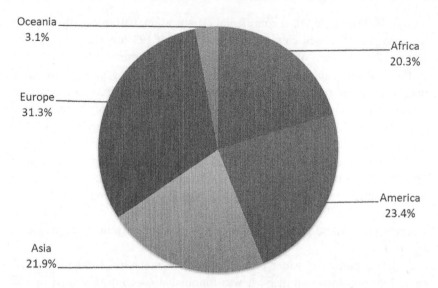

Figure 2. Countries with parliamentary involvement per continent.

small island states, at risk of disappearing due to climate change, one would expect that far more of them would have taken interest in conducting parliamentary control of the SDGs.

By early 2019, parliaments around the world had established 32 dedicated bodies to tackle SDG related challenges. Overall, it is calculated that of the 64 countries that have parliamentary involvement in the oversight of the SDGs, 32 have a dedicated parliamentary body. It is interesting to see whether these dedicated bodies are equally distributed around the globe. Unfortunately, they are not. Table 1 shows both the number of member states with parliamentary involvement per continent and those with dedicated parliamentary bodies. Hence, this metric shows the importance that is being vested in new institutions, such as a dedicated parliamentary body. One may notice that 10 out of 14 UN member states in Asia, a significant number, have a dedicated parliamentary body for the oversight of SDGs. *Vice versa*, none of the 2 member states in Oceania, e.g. Fiji and Samoa, have reported dedicated parliamentary bodies for the purpose.

Table 1. Countries with parliamentary involvement per continent.

Continent	# involvement	# bodies	%
Africa	13	5	38.5%
America	15	9	60.0%
Asia	14	10	71.4%
Europe	20	8	40.0%
Oceania	2	0	0.0%
Sum	64	32	

Note: Africa and Europe are below average (which is 50%); Asia and America are above average.

The analysis of the information about member states with a dedicated parliamentary body has led to five basic types of parliamentary bodies, which are depicted in Figure 3: Committees (16), Fora and Working Groups (9), Commissions (2), Task forces (2) and Ombudsman or commissioner (2).[6] The parliamentary bodies labelled as 'others' could not be categorised and included only Japan, where political party committees have been established to lead the dialogue on SDGs. The authors notice that half of the countries with dedicated parliamentary bodies, i.e. 16 out of 32, have chosen to establish a Committee or Sub-Committee. In some countries with bicameral parliaments, such as Nigeria and Spain, there are dedicated Committees in both Houses.

The findings also suggest a strong extra-parliamentary involvement, with 38 countries exercising one or more of its three facets: cooperation with government (14), multi-stakeholder dialogue (22) and participation to external commissions (7).[7] In total, these add up to 43 actions, meaning that some member states exercise more than one of these extra-parliamentary activities. 'Multi-stakeholder dialogue' (51.2 per cent) leads the relevant poll. 'Cooperation with government' comes second with 32.6 per cent, leaving 'participation to external commissions' third with 16.3 per cent. Finally, only 13 out of 153 member states, i.e. 8.5 per cent, were found to have internal procedures to exercise some level of control on budget issues related to SDGs.[8] Almost half of them, i.e. six out of 13, are located in America.

PLS for SDG monitoring

'The act of evaluating laws that a parliament has passed is known as Post Legislative Scrutiny' (PLS) (De Vrieze & Hasson, 2017). In the parliamentary domain, PLS falls under the function of parliamentary control (Norton, 2019). Nevertheless, to date, most parliaments lack sufficient capacity to

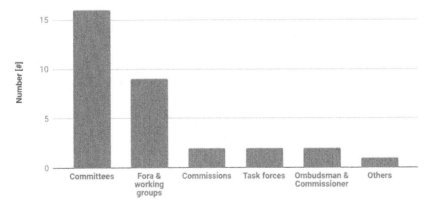

Figure 3. Types of established parliamentary bodies.

systematically follow up on the implementation of passed legislation. While the traditional system of – written or oral – questions is used by parliamentary groups and MPs to exercise parliamentary control, parliaments continue to build up their capacities in order to adapt to new challenges.

In early 2018, the Westminster Foundation for Democracy (WFD) completed a publication triplet on Post-Legislative Scrutiny (PLS). It now includes a comparative study of practices of PLS in selected parliaments (De Vrieze & Hasson, 2017), a guide for parliaments (De Vrieze, 2017) and a policy document with principles for PLS (De Vrieze, 2018). Analysis of case studies revealed a set of omnipresent principles that were documented in the relevant policy document. Further study displayed various options for introducing PLS into parliaments. These documents, and particularly the 'Guide for Parliaments' and the 'Principles', present the general framework for conducting PLS by parliaments and offer a solid methodology for implementation.

In general, PLS can be considered a broad concept along two main lines: the legal dimension assessing the enactment of the law and the impact dimension assessing to what extent the policy objectives of the law have been met. In this context, the possibility to apply PLS principles is examined to follow-up on the implementation of SDGs and to assess whether PLS is a viable long-term solution to guarantee their achievement. The choice of the PLS model is fundamental and the aforementioned comparative study may assist towards adopting the most appropriate one for any given parliamentary system. Nevertheless, it needs to be highlighted that PLS sometimes relies on solid 'information and reports provided by the government', although parliaments may also conduct own analysis (De Vrieze, 2017). Hence, all possible stakeholders need to come to an institutional agreement.

It is significant to underline that PLS is not only to be applied to single acts. This is particularly relevant when considering its application to the SDGs regime. As policy changes sometimes result from different laws, the recognition of the cumulative effect of legislation may encourage review of several laws at once, which are often related to one specific SDG. Another important issue is related to the timing and the duration of its application. Often, in the Westminster Parliament, PLS is conducted five years after enactment, while WFD principles mention a best practices time span of minimum three years. In other instances, this may happen even much later, as in the case of the Parliament of Nepal that initiated in April 2020 an in-depth PLS of the 1963 Infectious Diseases Act due to the COVID-19 pandemic. However, if there is sufficient evidence of the impact of the law(s), PLS can be conducted close to enactment. Usually, for a parliament, the most time-consuming part is to agree on the relevant framework. While in place, individual or sets of acts may be scrutinised in a pipelining manner. Hence, an individual PLS inquiry is possible to be conducted within a couple of months. Furthermore, it should be taken into consideration that SDGs might not be dependent on new legislation but rather on the application of existing acts. Hence, the PLS of existing legislation could provide evidence on where a country stands in achieving its SDG objectives.

The assignment of sufficient resources to conduct PLS is a prerequisite for its success. While it seems difficult to contract additional highly-skilled personnel (i.e. consultants) for conducting PLS, some parliaments assign PLS supporting duties to parliamentary research services, such as in South Korea (Cho, 2019). The extension of parliamentary research in the PLS domain certainly seems to be a viable solution, in particular for resource-scarce parliaments. Recent developments show that PLS is here to stay (De Vrieze, 2019; Griglio, 2019). Several parliaments implement PLS and a set of principles and best practice have already been recognised. If parliaments get it right, PLS has the potential to evolve into a stand-alone parliamentary function.

The above-mentioned set of principles is an important element of PLS and provides guidance in establishing a realistic framework for post-legislative practice, without neglecting current parliamentary legal and procedural practice (De Vrieze, 2018, p. 2). However, there are five specific principles that are particularly well suited to advance oversight of SDGs. These principles, from a to e, are presented below.

- Principle a: To assess the impact of legislation, it is useful to review secondary or delegated legislation at the same time as reviewing the primary act, or parent legislation.

Acts of parliament often grant ministers powers to make delegated or secondary legislation. It is ideal to review secondary legislation post-enactment at the same time as reviewing the parent legislation from which it owes its authority. This is particularly the case at times when most of the provisions giving effect to a piece of legislation are held within the secondary, rather than the primary legislation, and might lead to contradictions or gaps. In some parliaments, a committee on delegated powers and regulatory reform, or committee on regulations has been given this task, such as in Australia, Canada, Nepal, Sri Lanka and the UK. As with primary legislation, it would be open to parliamentary committees to commission research on the effect of specific secondary legislation or to undertake an inquiry. Applied to SDGs, this principle allows parliaments to delve into the increased complexity related to their oversight by analysing decrees and secondary legislation related to specific SDG fields, to what extent they are in line with primary legislation, do not infringe upon fundamental rights or aim for retro-active enactment not authorised by primary legislation.

- Principle b: PLS provides an opportunity to assess the impact of legislation on issues which cut across different Acts, such as on gender, on minorities, or on other vulnerable groups.

Legislative initiatives frequently affect men and women differently. Systematic analysis and evaluation of law and policy, based on how they impact women, men and other relevant demographic groups can help to identify and avert or redress any potential disadvantages they may create. Such analysis will help to ensure that women and men, and other vulnerable groups, have access to the same opportunities and legal protections. For instance, the Myanmar Parliament completed in 2019 a pilot project on PLS of the Children Law, highlighting implementation gaps and suggesting amendments to protect the youngest and most vulnerable in society. To undertake a gender analysis of the impact of legislation as relevant for the SDGs, there is a need for the collection of evidence, with sex-disaggregated data or qualitative assessments of government services. It also requires policy makers to challenge assumptions about how a government programme or service should be structured, and to ask detailed questions about who is affected by a problem or issue and how they would be impacted by proposed solutions. This principle ensures that the scrutiny of a multitude of legislative Acts takes into account the impact on gender and on the position of all vulnerable groups throughout different SDG policy fields.

- Principle c: Parliament should consider whether responsibility for PLS is assigned to its permanent Committees or to a dedicated body.

Who should conduct the PLS? In most parliaments, committees have the main responsibility for PLS as part of their oversight role. PLS thus needs to be placed in the work schedule of the Committees, in the agenda and work plan of Committees. Committees should not only review new legislation, but also PLS of past legislation. In some parliaments, the Legal or Legislative Committee conducts the review of the enactment of legislation, while the thematic committees assess the impact of the law. In some cases, the remit for PLS is explicitly assigned to a dedicated committee, as is Scotland and Lebanon. Regarding parliamentary monitoring of SDGs, each option has value; and the approach chosen depends on issues such as the rules of procedure; the appetite and the capacity of committees; parliament's oversight culture; established practices and the available human resources. The work of the Committee on Delegated Legislation and the Legislative Management Committee in the federal Parliament of Nepal is a good example (Sah et al., 2019). Moreover, the Parliament of Sri Lanka has a Committee on Evaluation which is now promoting a bill to advance the national evaluation capacity (Jayathilake & Tennakoon, 2019). In Myanmar, the law on microfinance has been scrutinised by the relevant Committee on Banks and Monetary Development (De Vrieze & Fitsilis, 2020).

- Principle d: For any parliament to conduct PLS inquiries efficiently and effectively, it needs to empower its human resources.

It is important for parliament to assign staff to work on PLS. It is usually the primary task of regular committee staff supported by the research department. There is need for parliaments to empower their staff with the requisite authority to interact with relevant institutions and stakeholders in the country and to collect the required information. Special care needs to be taken to train skilled personnel on PLS activities. Parliament may consider whether to establish a separate secretariat research service for PLS (as is the case in Indonesia and Switzerland). Alternatively, a parliament may also decide to commission an independent body or expert panel to carry out this legislative evaluation (as is the case in South Africa). Each approach has its rationale and its advantages; and it is up to the parliament leadership to decide which approach is most suitable within the specific national and parliamentary context. In addition, parliaments need to design and operate appropriate ICT systems and applications to capture, maintain and handle the necessary data to perform PLS activities. Again, this principle is in-line with the necessary actions to efficiently monitor SDGs, to which belongs the strengthening of the capacity and resources of parliamentary staff.

- Principle e: It is useful when PLS can rely on official information, but it also needs the views and information of a wide range of stakeholders, including civil society organisations.

Beyond official, government information, public engagement in PLS enables access to additional sources of information, increases the credibility of findings and enhances public trust in democratic institutions. Public consultation and engagement can enhance public trust in parliament and the democratic institutions in general. The results of the PLS findings, such as the PLS report, need to be publicly accessible, preferably using open data and document standards (such as in the UK). The central position of parliaments in a democratic governance system enables them to directly access reliable information from all relevant stakeholders, on the one side and to efficiently communicate the results of its oversight activity, on the other. Hence, this PLS principle is of increased added value when applied in order to monitor SDGs. The Environment Committee of the Parliament of the Republic of Georgia conducted in 2019 a PLS on legislation regarding electric cars and engaged a wide group of professional associations, civil society, industry and environmental activists, enabling it to put forward a solid report with recommendations, directly upscaling the country's alignment with the relevant SDGs regarding the environment (Kuchava, 2019).

Conclusion and outlook

This article is the first comprehensive review of parliamentary involvement in relation to the monitoring of the implementation of SDGs, based upon quantitative data. The analysis of the information regarding national or federal parliaments of UN member states has led to the determination of a set of basic types of dedicated parliamentary bodies that handle SDG related issues. Moreover, the nature of cooperation with extra-parliamentary stakeholders, such as the Government, NGOs and international organisations (IOs) is closely analysed. In summary, to the most significant results belong the following:

- 79.3% (=153/193) of the UN member states were examined,
- 41.8% (=64/153) of the countries display parliamentary involvement,
- of which, 50% (=32/64) are the countries with dedicated parliamentary bodies,
- 20.9% (=32/153) of the examined countries have dedicated parliamentary bodies.

These are already remarkably high results of parliamentary involvement that are surely going to improve during 2019 and 2020, as the announced VNRs start to get published. At this point, it needs to be underlined that the existence of a parliamentary working body dedicated to the SDGs is merely a strong indicator of the determination of a parliament to actively engage in SDG monitoring. It does not constitute *per se* a quality indicator of parliamentary involvement.

The Indonesian Parliament, for instance, has not formed a special committee or sub-committee on SDGs, but rather assigns the task under the existing standing committees. The Inter-Parliamentary Cooperation Committee has been chosen to coordinate the parliamentary works on SDGs because the parliament considers SDGs as a UN led initiative, hence it is seen as international affairs. Through this committee, the parliament has organised a number of high-profile international fora on SDGs, which have benefitted from the PLS resources of the Indonesian parliament.[9] In Finland, there is a similar case. These exists no dedicated parliamentary committee on SDGs, but the parliament is widely represented in two significant governmental committees: the National Commission on Sustainable Development and the Development Policy Committee. The parliamentary Committee for the Future oversees overall implementation of Agenda 2030 (Berg et al., 2019). Hence, where no information of parliamentary involvement is to be found it is rather straightforward to assume that the standard parliamentary control procedure via 'line committees' is used to scrutinise SDGs.

The findings show that parliaments rarely deal with budgetary issues related to the implementation of SDGs, i.e. in less than 10 per cent (=13/153) of the examined countries. The role of parliaments in monitoring allocation of budget in relation to SDGs could be significant, particularly in cases where a Parliamentary Budget Office (PBO) is already or in the process of being established, as in Montenegro and Ukraine. Certainly, not all parliaments are equally forthcoming when it comes to SDGs. Some restrict their involvement to informative measures towards MPs, e.g. through trainings, sometimes with the help of third parties such as IPU and UNDP. This is for example the case in Brazil and Samoa.

Can PLS increase the efficiency of SDG monitoring and, consequently, implementation? The answer can only be affirmative, for three reasons:

- First, because PLS is based on a series of principles that are well-suited to follow-up on the progress of SDGs. In this regard, the proven PLS framework offers a series of tools and practices to assist parliaments. However, parliaments need first to determine a clear PLS concept.[10] Through it, additional momentum may be generated to policy and law makers to amend existing primary and secondary legislation and advance its quality. Within the PLS framework, new creative ways of parliamentary scrutiny may be established. PLS actors can make use of *de facto* significant parliamentary visibility to address and localise SDG related issues.
- Second, SDG monitoring is about monitoring the impact of policies and policy commitments, which are often and to a large extent based in legislation. Assessing the impact of legislation through PLS thus constitutes a vehicle that feeds into the SDG monitoring. This is most obvious in SDG related legislation, such as the mentioned law on the rights of the child in Myanmar. Monitoring progress in this type of SDG policy areas requires monitoring the impact of the related legislation, hence creating a direct link between the PLS approach and the SDGs.
- Third, while any PLS process requires a minimum timeframe for identifying weaknesses in legislation, proposing changes, and then amending the original bill or introducing a new one, for any substantial policies in the area of the SDGs to be sustainable for years to come, they need to have a solid legal basis; and the absence of a fitting legal framework has been one of the weaknesses in making progress towards achieving the SDGs by 2030. Therefore, the PLS instrument, while not being a fast track mechanism for SDG implementation, can exactly provide a firm basis for the required firm legal framework by enabling policies contributing to achieving the SDGs.

Despite offering novel insights into the parliamentary involvement in SDG monitoring, several things still need to be done to upgrade the existing dataset, widen the scope of research and make it more useful to all stakeholders. First, the time dimension needs to be added, i.e. the assessment needs to be repeated in a two-year cycle until 2030. It is at hand that this presents a huge task, difficult to be carried out by a single group of researchers. In addition, while studying VNRs in detail, non-scientific phrasing and discrepancies in reporting could be visible.

For a unified collection of quantitative and textual data, the authors propose the development of a web platform in which national contact points from member states would directly enter their progress in distinct time frames and in a more controlled fashion.[11] Moreover, advanced training – other than preparatory workshops – is needed for those who draft VNRs, maybe through an e-learning procedure (e-learning tool). A UN level task force, e.g. under the UN Department for Economic and Social Affairs, Division for Public Administration and Development Management, could also be established for express web and field assistance.

Notes

1. The study, as well as some of its basic findings, were first announced at the Academic Conference on Post-Legislative Scrutiny in Asia, on 17–18 June 2019, which took place in Yangon, Myanmar; an early conference version was presented at Wroxton, UK; see also Fitsilis and De Vrieze (2019); the two-dimensional matrix contains data on countries, intra-and extra-parliamentary conduct, control of the SDG budget and general comments; the dataset has been published in early 2019 and includes data entries also for the states that have chosen to submit a VNR in 2019 and 2020; consequently, no special data on parliamentary involvement are available for these countries; nevertheless they are included in the country statistics.
2. The actual question as to whether budget alignment is necessary to meet SDG related targets requires special attention and is going to be tackled in follow-up contributions.
3. Besides scarcity, there are publications dealing with potential benefits from parliamentary involvement, rather than analysing actual conduct; see, e.g. Datta and Rabbany (2016), who analyse the potential of parliamentary involvement in Bangladesh.
4. This work can be also considered to belong to the realm of meta-studies, as it tries to synthesise the findings of multiple sources; in IPU (2019), institutionalisation of SDGs is also tackled, but using a significantly different methodology, i.e. by using a survey, thus complicating direct comparison of results; in addition, IPU uses its concept of geopolitical groups.
5. According to the geographical classification used, Cyprus, as an EU member state, belongs to Europe, rather than Asia; Palestine, which has UN observer status, is part of the dataset, but was not included in the calculations.

6. The 'Committee type' also includes sub-committees, since they rely on the same basic principle; fora and working groups are networks consisted of Members of Parliament (MPs).
7. Reference is made to institutionalised cooperation between government and parliament on SDGs; typical stakeholders may include professional chambers, Civil Society Organizations (CSOs), Non-Governmental Organizations (NGOs), local self-governments and others.
8. These member states are: Norway, Finland, Montenegro, Uruguay, Ecuador, Costa Rica, Guatemala, Peru, Honduras, Sudan, Uganda, Mali and Nigeria.
9. See, for example, the 1st, 2nd and 3rd World Parliamentary Forum on Sustainable Development in 2017, 2018 and 2019, respectively.
10. Parliaments may exercise PLS via commission, committee, an external working body, independent state body or otherwise.
11. One can also think of fully-standardised dynamic VNRs, in the form of akoma ntoso-based legal documents (Sartor et al., 2011); such documents would have the advantage of being possible to evaluate in real time.

Acknowledgements

Many thanks go to Agus Wijayanto for providing operational insights of the Indonesian Parliament, and to Eleni Zisioglou and Dimitris Garantziotis of the *Hellenic OCR Team*, for their invaluable assistance in conducting the word study on SDGs and in drafting of the present text, respectively.

Disclosure statement

No potential conflict of interest was reported by the author(s).

ORCID

Fotios Fitsilis http://orcid.org/0000-0003-1531-4128
Franklin De Vrieze http://orcid.org/0000-0001-5054-1313

References

ALDA. (2016). The SDGs in a few lines: The origin, the state of play and the objectives. European Association for Local Democracy. Retrieved July 5, 2019, from http://www.ladder-project.eu/wp-content/uploads/2016/04/The-SDGs-in-a-glance.pdf

Berg, A., Lähteenoja, S., Ylönen, M., Korhonen-Kurki, K., Linko, T., Lonkila, K.-M., ... Suutarinen, I. (2019). PATH2030 – An evaluation of Finland's sustainable development policy publications of the government's analysis, assessment and research activities 23/2019. Retrieved August 2, 2019, from https://www.demoshelsinki.fi/wp-content/uploads/2019/05/path2030-an-evaluation-of-finlands-sustainable-development-policy.pdf

Cho, S. (2019). *The role of legislative support agencies for legislative impact analysis in South Korea: Focusing on NABO and NARS* [Paper presentation]. Academic Conference on Post-Legislative Scrutiny, June, 17–18. Yangon, Myanmar. Manuscript in preparation.

Datta, S. K., & Rabbany, H. (2016). Sustainable development goals and Bangladesh: The role of parliament. *International Journal of Development Research*, 6(7), 8599–8606.

De Vrieze, F. (2017). Post-legislative scrutiny guide for parliaments. WFD. Retrieved July 5, 2019, from https://www.wfd.org/wp-content/uploads/2018/07/WFD_Manual-on-Post-Legislative-Scrutiny.pdf

De Vrieze, F. (2018). Principles of post-legislative scrutiny by parliaments. WFD. Retrieved July 5, 2019, from https://www.wfd.org/wp-content/uploads/2018/07/Principles-of-Post-Legislative-Scrutiny-by-Parliaments.pdf

De Vrieze, F. (2019). Introduction. *European Journal of Law Reform*, 21(2), 3–4. https://doi.org/10.5553/EJLR/138723702019021002001

De Vrieze, F., & Fitsilis, F. (2020). Applying post-legislative scrutiny to the analysis of legislation and SDGs in South and Southeast Asia. Manuscript submitted for publication.

De Vrieze, F., & Hasson, V. (2017). Comparative study of practices of post-legislative scrutiny in selected parliaments and the rationale for its place in democracy assistance. WFD. Retrieved July 5, 2019, from https://www.wfd.org/wp-content/uploads/2018/07/Comparative-Study-PLS-WEB.pdf

Deveaux, K., & Rodrigues, C. (2018). Parliament's role in implementing the sustainable development goals – a parliamentary handbook. GOPAC, UNDP and IDB. Retrieved July 5, 2019, from https://www.undp.org/content/dam/undp/library/Democratic%20Governance/Parliamentary%20Development/parliaments%20role%20in%20implementing%20the%20SDGs.pdf

European Commission. (2016). Next steps for a sustainable European future – European action for sustainability. Communication from the Commission to the EUP, the Council the European Economic and Social Committee and the Committee of the Regions. SWD(2016) 390 final. Retrieved July 5, 2019, from https://ec.europa.eu/europeaid/sites/devco/files/communication-next-steps-sustainable-europe-20161122_en.pdf

Eurostat. (2019). Sustainable development goals – overview. Retrieved July 8, 2019, from https://ec.europa.eu/eurostat/web/sdi/overview

Fitsilis, F., & De Vrieze, F. (2019). Parliamentary oversight of sustainable development goals and the application of post-legislative scrutiny principles. 14th Workshop of Parliamentary Scholars and Parliamentarians, Wroxton, UK, 27–28 July. Retrieved August 30, 2019, from https://doi.org/10.2139/ssrn.3429635

Fitsilis, F., & Zisioglou, E. (2019). Dataset on parliamentary involvement in SDG monitoring. *Figshare.* https://doi.org/10.6084/m9.figshare.7945628.v2

Griglio, E. (2019). Post-legislative scrutiny as a form of executive oversight: Tools and practices in Europe. *European Journal of Law Reform, 21*(2), 36–54. https://doi.org/10.5553/EJLR/138723702019021002004

HLPF. (2019). High-level political forum on sustainable development (n.d.). Retrieved July 8, 2019, from https://sustainabledevelopment.un.org/hlpf/2019/

House of Commons. (2016). UK Implementation of the SDGs. International Development Committee. Retrieved July 5, 2019, from https://publications.parliament.uk/pa/cm201617/cmselect/cmintdev/103/103.pdf

ICLEI. (2015). From MDGS to SDGS: What are the sustainable development goals? Urban Issues 1. Retrieved July 5, 2019, from http://localizingthesdgs.org/library/251/From-MDGs-to-SDGs-What-are-the-Sustainable-Development-Goals.pdf

IPU. (2016). Parliaments and the sustainable development goals, a self-assessment toolkit. Retrieved July 5, 2019, from https://www.ipu.org/resources/publications/handbooks/2017-01/parliaments-and-sustainable-development-goals-self-assessment-toolkit

IPU. (2018). Sustainable development goals. Retrieved July 5, 2019, from https://www.ipu.org/our-work/sustainable-development/sustainable-development-goals

IPU. (2019). Institutionalization of the sustainable development goals in the work of parliaments. Retrieved July 31, 2019, from https://www.ipu.org/sites/default/files/documents/sdg_survey_analysis-final-e.pdf

Jayathilake, T. K., & Tennakoon, N. (2019). *Policy and legislation evaluation and scrutiny by parliament of Sri Lanka: The way forward* [Paper presentation] Academic Conference on Post-Legislative Scrutiny, June, 17–18. Yangon, Myanmar. Manuscript in preparation.

Kuchava, K. (2019). First post-legislative scrutiny in Georgia: Steps towards generating result-oriented Laws. *Journal of Southeast Asian Human Rights, 3*(2), 258–276. https://doi.org/10.19184/jseahr.v3i2.13600

Mulholland, E. (2017). The role of European parliaments in the implementation of the 2030 Agenda and the SDGs. ESDN Quarterly Report 45. Retrieved July 5, 2019, from https://www.sd-network.eu/quarterly%20reports/report%20files/pdf/2017-July-The_Role_of_European_Parliaments_in_the_Implementation_of_the_2030_Agenda_and_the_SDGs.pdf

Nelson, E. (2018). The US and Russia are doing the least to achieve the UN's sustainable development goals. Retrieved July 5, 2019, from https://qz.com/1328895/unsustainable-development-goals-the-us-and-russia-are-doing-the-least-among-g20-nations/

Norton, P. (2019). Post-legislative scrutiny in the UK parliament: Adding value. *The Journal of Legislative Studies,* https://doi.org/10.1080/13572334.2019.1633778

Power, G. (2012). *The changing nature of parliamentary representation (First Global Parliamentary Report).* Geneva, New York: IPU & UNDP. Retrieved July 5, 2019. http://archive.ipu.org/pdf/publications/gpr2012-full-e.pdf

Robert, K. W., Parris, T. M., & Leiserowitz, A. A. (2005). What is sustainable development? Goals, indicators, values, and practice. *Environment: Science and Policy for Sustainable Development, 47*(3), 8–21. Retrieved July 5, 2019, from https://sites.hks.harvard.edu/sustsci/ists/docs/whatisSD_env_kates_0504.pdf https://doi.org/10.1080/00139157.2005.10524444

Sachs, J., Schmidt-Traub, G., Kroll, C., Lafortune, G., & Fuller, G. (2018). *SDG Index and Dashboards report 2018.* Bertelsmann Stiftung and Sustainable Development Solutions Network (SDSN).

Sachs, J., Schmidt-Traub, G., Kroll, C., Lafortune, G., & Fuller, G. (2019). *Sustainable development report 2019*. Bertelsmann Stiftung and Sustainable Development Solutions Network (SDSN).

Sah, R. K., Mahato, S., & Chaudhary, P. (2019). *Legislators' engagement in policy making and post-legislative scrutiny in Nepalese parliament since 1991* [Paper presentation]. Academic Conference on Post-Legislative Scrutiny, June 17–18, Yangon, Myanmar. Manuscript in preparation.

Sartor, G., Palmirani, M., Francesconi, E., & Biasiotti, M. A. eds. (2011). *Legislative XML for the semantic web: Principles, models, standards for document management (vol. 4)*. Springer.

SDG16 Hub. (2019). Retrieved July 5, 2019, from https://www.sdg16hub.org/parliaments

TAP Network. (2016). Goal 16 advocacy toolkit. Retrieved July 5, 2019, from https://tapnetwork2030.org/wp-content/uploads/2016/07/TAP_AdvocacyToolkit_1pgFINAL.pdf

Together 2030. (2018). Engaging parliaments on the 2030 Agenda and the SDGs: Representation, accountability and implementation. Retrieved July 5, 2019, from http://www.partners-for-review.de/wp-content/uploads/2018/12/Engaging-parliaments-on-the-2030-Agenda-and-the-SDGs.pdf

Trihartono, A., Patriadi, H. B., & Hara, A. E. (2019). The role of government in post-legislative scrutiny: Case study of revision to the fisheries law in Indonesia [Paper presentation]. Academic Conference on Post-Legislative Scrutiny, June 17–18. Yangon, Myanmar. Manuscript in preparation.

UN. (2015). Transforming our world: The 2030 agenda for sustainable development. General Assembly Resolution A/RES/70/1. Retrieved July 5, 2019, from https://www.un.org/en/development/desa/population/migration/generalassembly/docs/globalcompact/A_RES_70_1_E.pdf

UN. (2018a). The sustainable development goals report 2018. Retrieved July 5, 2019, from https://unstats.un.org/sdgs/files/report/2018/TheSustainableDevelopmentGoalsReport2018-EN.pdf

UN. (2018b). Compendium of National Institutional Arrangements for implementing the 2030 Agenda for Sustainable Development. UN Department for Economic and Social Affairs Division for Public Administration and Development Management. Retrieved July 5, 2019, from http://workspace.unpan.org/sites/Internet/Documents/UNPAN97468.pdf

UN. (2019a). SDGs knowledge platform. Retrieved July 5, 2019, from https://sustainabledevelopment.un.org/sdgs

UN. (2019b). Sustainable development knowledge platform. Retrieved July 5, 2019, from https://sustainabledevelopment.un.org/unsystem

World Commission on Environment and Development. (1987). *Our common future (\'Brundtland report\')*. New York: United Nations. Retrieved July 5, 2019, from http://www.un-documents.net/wced-ocf.htm

Towards parliamentary full cycle engagement in the legislative process: innovations and challenges

Jonathan Murphy

ABSTRACT
As representative democracy has come under criticism from populists and advocates of 'participatory democracy', parliaments have responded by expanding their engagements throughout the governance process. Parliaments around the world are participating in the development of policy proposals including in dialogue with citizens, the shaping of draft legislation, debate and adoption of legislative proposals, in post-legislative scrutiny, and in government oversight and audit. The article explores the motivators for these enhanced roles, the opportunities and challenges entailed in a parliamentary full-cycle approach, and makes recommendations for parliaments and parliamentary development actors to enable successful implementation of an expanded and deepened role for parliaments as core institutions of representative democracy.

Introduction[1]

Parliaments are playing an increasingly central role in governance processes. Whereas many parliaments formerly operated in the shadow of powerful executives, today parliaments in both established and emerging democracies are assuming a more prominent place throughout the legislative – and indeed broader governance – cycle. This phenomenon seems to derive from a variety of different factors. These include increased demands by citizens for their MPs to play an autonomous role rather than just act as a voting bank for their party,[2] and the growth of independent institutions supporting parliament which provide deeper analysis to MPs and thus redress the information asymmetry between executive and legislature. This meshes with the general societal trend for more transparent governance, for which parliamentary processes are well-suited, given that deliberations often take place in public and frequently provide opportunities for civil society, expert, and citizen input.

The growing tendency towards full cycle engagement in the legislative process, with parliaments engaged from conceptualisation to adoption to post-legislative scrutiny and audit, is marked by increased use of consultative processes. These vary widely according to jurisdiction, but can include green and white papers, the introduction of regulatory impact assessments as part of legislative scrutiny, and the expanded use of post-legislative scrutiny as a consistent part of parliamentary work. These enhancements in parliament's work enable a more coherent and responsible process, whereby parliament is engaged through the full policy process, thus integrating legislative scrutiny with oversight, and feeding back into the cycle of policy development and refinement.

The growing engagement of parliaments in governance is not, however, without its challenges and its critics. Some argue that parliament has assumed functions best carried out by the executive, which is better staffed and technically equipped to carry out detailed analysis, and more insulated from constituent demands (Lienert, 2010, p. 19; Wehner, 2010). Others argue that parliament is beginning to encroach on executive prerogatives and make societies ungovernable (Häkkinen, 2014); a British prime minister recently made such a claim in regard to that country's 'Brexit' process.[3]

It is argued in this article that parliaments' increasing ubiquity throughout the policy process reflects much more than a push-back against policy technicity on one hand, or an unwarranted encroachment on executive privilege on the other. Rather, the increased demands on parliament and parliaments' growing willingness to respond to those demands signify an expansion of the scope of representative democracy, in response to, among other factors, the twin challenges of populism[4] and demands for participatory and deliberative democracy.

The article begins by exploring some of the pressures that are leading parliaments to move towards 'full cycle' governance engagements. It then examines the broader societal dynamics that underpin this shift to more activist parliaments. It explores some of the challenges that parliaments face in taking on these new roles in areas such as pre-legislative consultations (e.g. Brazier, 2004; Tellier, 2015), regulatory impact assessment (Radaelli & De Francesco, 2010), and post-legislative scrutiny (Norton, 2019). It then goes on to look at some of the limitations and risks in this expanded parliamentary role. Next, the article explores three specific case studies of parliaments that have been early movers in extended engagement in the legislative cycle, in the Republic of Georgia, in Scotland, and in South Africa. It highlights examples of successes as well as challenges that have arisen in these cases. Finally, some conclusions are drawn on the conditions required for expanded engagement of legislatures in the policy process to enhance governance. This is a developmental paper that aims to situate the emergence of greater parliamentary engagement within a broader analytical framework.

Parliaments' full cycle governance ambitions

Many parliaments' engagement in governance has deepened considerably over the past two decades, and extended across the governance cycle. In the past, many parliaments were accused of being just 'rubber stamps' for all-powerful executives (Barkan, 2005). For example, they were often accused of carrying out only cursory scrutiny of legislative proposals to be passed along party lines (Lester, 2002), and in their financial oversight role, of depending excessively upon supreme audit institutions for a primarily compliance-oriented, rather than performance-based, audit of government expenditures (Johnson & Talbot, 2007).

Now, parliaments are making serious efforts to participate throughout the policy development and implementation cycle, with the implicit or explicit objective of a 'joined-up' approach that ensures knowledge and insights gained in one stage of parliament's work, are then taken into account at future stages of parliamentary involvement. This approach responds to a common criticism of parliaments, that they vote laws and budgets without paying serious attention to the impact of legislation or the effectiveness of state financing; thus, exercising power without responsibility.[5]

What factors are driving the change towards a more extensive and intensive parliamentary engagement? In this article, it is argued that there are both overt factors leading to greater parliamentary engagement, and deeper underlying shifts in understandings and expectations of representative democracy. In this section, we will explore some of the overt factors that encourage more activist parliaments engaging throughout the legislative cycle. In the next section, we will explore some of the underlying changes in perceptions of the meaning of representative democracy. While these two types of factors appear conceptually different, the article presents the hypothesis that shifts in broader expectations of democracy tend naturally to lead to the specific expansions of parliamentary roles discussed in this article (Figure 1).

Probably the most decisive overt factor in parliament's assumption of a more prominent role in governance, is a far greater level of exigency on the part of citizens. In most democratic countries, opinion surveys suggest that citizens demand both greater engagement *with* parliament, and also greater accountability *of* parliament (Power, 2012, pp. 21–22). Surveys also show quite consistently that parliaments and parliamentarians tend to be among the least trusted institutions and elites respectively (Leston-Bandeira, 2012; Lewis, 2002; Whitmore, 2019). In response, parliamentarians naturally seek to find ways to demonstrate their effectiveness and to improve their public image; one way to achieve this is through deeper and more visible engagement in strengthening parliament's role in effective governance.

A supply-led factor that has enabled parliaments to be more active through the policy cycle is the burgeoning number of independent oversight

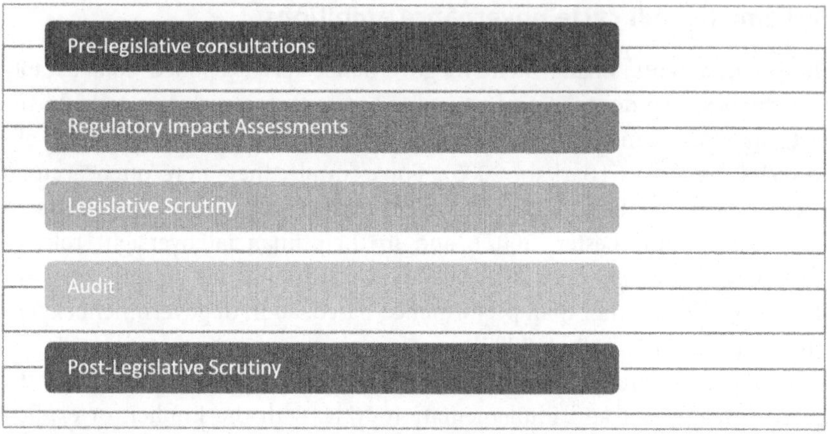

```
┌─────────────────────────────────────────┐
│     Pre-legislative consultations       │
├─────────────────────────────────────────┤
│     Regulatory Impact Assessments       │
├─────────────────────────────────────────┤
│     Legislative Scrutiny                │
├─────────────────────────────────────────┤
│     Audit                               │
├─────────────────────────────────────────┤
│     Post-Legislative Scrutiny           │
└─────────────────────────────────────────┘
```

Figure 1. Entry points for full cycle parliamentary engagement.

institutions,[6] normally reporting fully or in part to parliament (Murphy & De Vrieze, 2020). While supreme audit institutions have existed in most countries for many years, a network of new bodies has emerged in many countries including human rights ombuds offices and commissions, anti-corruption bodies, access to information and privacy commissioners, etc. For example, the number of national ombuds institutions increased from 29 in 1980 to 45 in 1990, 100 in 2000, and 133 in 2000.[7] While many of these bodies have roles to accept complaints from citizens and carry out investigations in their mandate areas, they almost all also have a broader role to assess overall conditions and reform needs, and to submit reports to parliament. This provides parliament with detailed information enabling parliament both to enhance its own oversight work and to ensure effective follow-up on independent institution recommendations.

Pressure from 'democratic competition'; civil society in all its diverse forms, has also spurred parliaments to a greater level of policy cycle engagement. The growing role of civil society organisations – whose activities are often defined as 'participatory democracy' – is frequently presented as an alternative to representative democracy that is regularly castigated as elite-captured and out of touch with citizen concerns (Naidoo, 2003; Scholte, 2004). While during the rise of civil society from the 1970s, parliamentarians often reacted defensively towards civil society,[8] most parliamentarians have understood that, while there will always be frictions around their comparative legitimacy, civil society and parliament can complement each other, particularly in providing knowledge to feed into the legislative and oversight processes (Burns, 1999; Doherty, 2001).

Another factor that has pushed parliament into deeper policy engagement is a general trend within governance for demonstrable outcomes (Henman,

2016; Lynch & Day, 1996). Increasingly, public service programming comes with measurable goals that are integrated into reporting (Verbeeten & Speklé, 2015); parliament thus has ready access to information about programme effectiveness, and a stronger foundation to carry out oversight through holding officials to account where there is a gap between goal and outcome.

Finally, the development of parliamentary norms has been a motivating factor from within the parliamentary community (O'Brien et al., 2016). The global Inter-Parliamentary Union (Beetham, 2006) as well as sub-global parliamentary organisations such as the Commonwealth Parliamentary Association (Commonwealth Parliamentary Association, 2018), the Association Parlementaire de la Francophonie (Assemblée Parlementaire de la Francophonie, 2009), and the Southern Africa Development Community Parliamentary Forum (SADAC-PF) (SADC Parliamentary Forum, 2010) have all developed norms and benchmarks. Mainly intended for self-assessment, they focus parliaments' attention on international best practices, and thus, on areas where reform would benefit the functioning and status of parliament. All of these benchmarks favour an integrated engagement of parliament through the policy cycle.

In the next section, we will briefly explore some of the underlying changes in conceptions of representative democracy that appear to foster this greater parliamentary activism.

Challenges and opportunities for renewing representative democracy

The past few years have been marked by paradoxical developments in democratic governance. On the one hand, many of the most stable liberal democracies have been challenged by the rise of populist movements which, even if not overtly hostile to the idea of democracy, privilege authoritarian solutions to the perceived dysfunctionalities of current governance. Such an attitude is most eloquently reflected in Hungarian Prime Minister Viktor Orban's rallying cry for an 'illiberal democracy' (Pap, 2017), which appears to be a democracy shorn of universalist pretensions and predicated on the concentration of power in the hands of an executive empowered through a plebiscitary, winner-takes-all electoral process. Other more insurrectionary movements, such as France's *Gilets Jaunes*, channel dissatisfaction without necessarily proposing clear alternatives to the status quo.

On the other hand, recent years have seen unprecedented demands for citizen engagement in decision-making processes, expressed in a variety of ways. On one end of the spectrum, there has been a burgeoning of street protests calling for radical policy reform, most if not all organised around campaigns of civil disobedience, ranging from Occupy Wall Street to Extinction

Rebellion. On the other, deliberative, end of the spectrum, there are numerous initiatives aiming to find ways to engage citizens in policy development processes, such as citizen's conventions,[9] mooted for example as a means to resolve the impasse in Britain over Brexit.

While the different challenges and threats have little in common in terms of policy solutions, it is generally accepted that they arise and draw support from generally declining deference, as well as growing citizen dissatisfaction – at both ends of the political spectrum – with what is perceived as an exclusionary homogeneity of post-ideological politics. If Fukuyama's (2006) *End of History* could be considered the slogan of the apogee of the third wave of democratisations of the 1980s and early 1990s, the multiple and diverse movements of contestation of the 2010s represent a clear rebuttal of such an eternal 'business as usual'.

Renewing thinking about representative democracy

Although rarely discussed explicitly in an era in which expertise is denigrated, the changing expectations of citizens and the growing demands on parliaments derive from a gradual shift in underlying beliefs regarding democracy; from a minimalist conception, in which we simply elect leaders who will make decisions on our behalf, to a procedural view in which representative democracy includes two central features; deliberation, and the vote (Urbinati, 2006). This view of representative democracy as a 'diarchy' is theoretically associated with both Nadia Urbinati (2016), and Kari Palonen (2016). Urbinati (2016) summarises the procedural view thus:

> Diarchic proceduralism accounts for the circularity of communication between the inside and the outside of state institutions, government and society, decision and opinion. It conceives democracy as a way of dealing with citizens' need to revise certainties and strategies of knowledge in order to be better capable of adjusting their decisions to new situations and of being receptive of others' experience. (p. 229)

By clearly understanding and articulating a vision for representative democracy that corresponds with the interiorised expectation of contemporary citizens, we are able to propose approaches that at the same time both assert the primacy of citizens in the democratic process (not simply signing over their power for four or five years as proposed by a minimalist view of democracy), and give life to the process of 'communication between the inside and the outside of state institutions' (Urbinati, 2012, p. 661). While this communication and deliberation can occur in various formats and structures, parliaments, at a national level at least, are both formally, and in practice, the preferred location. Democratically elected parliaments represent the diversity of a population, are accountable to citizens and in turn, hold the executive accountable, and combine deliberation with formal decision-making.

Building from this vision of the roles of contemporary parliaments enables us to conceptualise expanded parliamentary functioning in terms of broader democratic objectives, rather than as a self-interested ruse to create a more elaborate, complex and less responsive system, as populist leaders regularly assert when parliament puts brakes on illiberal reforms.

For deliberation to be effectively connected to the vote – parliamentary decision-making – it is critical that parliaments should have real insight into the overall governance process, from discussion of the principles of proposed legislation, through to scrutiny of the legislation, monitoring and oversight of its implementation, and ultimately, post-facto audit. In this way, citizens' interests and perspectives are represented not only in the initial ex-ante consideration of the merits of different policy and regulatory approaches, but also through the chance to 're-deliberate' once the results are in. Thus, a more engaged parliament helps to fulfil Urbinati's injunction that democracy must address, 'citizens' need to revise certainties and strategies of knowledge in order to be better capable of adjusting their decisions to new situations' (Figure 2).

If we consider the practical implications of such an approach, these represent both an opportunity and a challenge for parliament. An opportunity, because parliament is now able to follow legislation throughout its life cycle, and a challenge because this expanded role requires considerably more effort and resources than earlier models in which legislative scrutiny

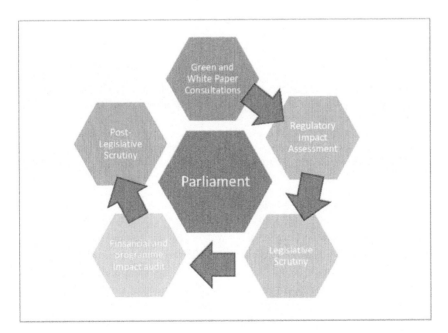

Figure 2. A model of Parliamentary full cycle engagement.

and post-facto audit were largely separate, with little feedback from (a largely financial) audit to enhanced policy implementation or legislative revision.

The populist challenge

Further consideration needs to be given to the populist challenge, which is reflected both inside and outside parliament. While parliament, like any state institution, should seek above all to do good – in other words, to enhance the possibility for citizens to live in freedom and harmony – it must also consider how its actions correspond to the expectations of citizens, as well as to the anticipated critiques of opponents of procedural, institutionalised democracy.

Although there are exceptions, populists are typically little interested in what they see as the technical minutiae of governance. They prefer to appeal to sweeping generalisation, hyperbole, and simple solutions. To the extent that populists are interested in parliamentary deliberations, this is mainly as a stage to enact theatre and to denounce the effete irrelevance of procedures that a decisive strong man could simply cut through like a knife through butter.

Thus, one leading populist used the European Parliament plenary session to dismiss the EU president as having,

> all the charisma of a damp rag and the appearance of a low-grade bank clerk ... "I have no doubt that your intention is to be the quiet assassin of European democracy and of European nation states."[10]

As for deliberation, the same populist parliamentarian stated to the European Parliament in regard to Brexit,

> We don't want to waste four more years of our life. Four more years of agony. You don't want to waste four more years. You've got your plan. You want your United States of Europe. You want your army. You want the Euro. You want to get rid of the nation state. We are just a damn nuisance. You don't want me coming back here and hoards of Euro sceptics coming back here.... We leave and both you and we can get on with the rest of our lives. That is the only neat solution ahead of us.[11]

A deliberative parliament engaged throughout the policy cycle needs, therefore, to be aware and ready to respond to this critique of endless timewasting, when 'decisiveness' could apparently immediately resolve any issue. Such decisiveness in populist governance could be invested in the role of the Leader; or in more democratic iterations, the people through plebiscites; or, in a favoured combination, a plebiscite granting the Leader the authority to be decisive. Ironically, the more exhaustively inclusive the parliamentary institution, the more it will be attacked as irrelevant to the citizens it is attempting to engage.

There is no sure defence or magic bullet to the populist critique. Parliaments and polities that have been relatively effective in limiting the impacts of populism do tend to be those that have invested strategically and significantly in both dialogic processes, and civic education (rather than simply communication). Examples include the parliaments of the Republic of Ireland,[12] and of Scotland.[13]

Ultimately, however, the most effective approach to populism is authenticity in engagement and approaches throughout the legislative and oversight cycle that represent real opportunities for participation in the decision-making process and not merely a *mise en scène*. Too often, there has been some validity in citizen scepticism regarding participatory processes, in which either the options are restricted to those considered desirable by the organisers of the process, and/or the mere fact of participation, even if views are not taken into account, is claimed to reflect consent in whatever decision is ultimately made (Cooke & Kothari, 2001).

In response to this legitimate concern, some of the parliaments most committed to effective citizen engagement have introduced provisions in their rules of procedure that require reports from consultative processes to include both a summary of inputs that have been received from citizens, experts, and interest groups; and, a statement of how inputs have contributed to the decisions ultimately taken.

Parliaments begin accepting a growing role in a more complex governance environment

Parliaments' initial responses to growing demands for a more open and responsive political system were often quite negative. Parliamentarians would frequently compare their electoral mandates from thousands of electors, to the civil society organisations that they classified as 'self-appointed'. However, such easy dismissal became much less simple once populists of various complexions were elected to parliaments and even presidencies, promising in a variety of often contradictory ways to 'return power to the people'.

In the past few years, parliaments in both established and emerging democracies have made serious efforts to both operate more openly and interactively with citizens, and also to expand parliament's roles beyond the sometimes ceremonial functions that appeared to predominate in the later neoliberal era, particularly in majoritarian polities with strong party discipline. On one hand, parliamentarians have – often grudgingly – accepted greater transparency in their conduct. On the other hand, they have increasingly assumed a much more independent role than the rubber stamp for executive decisions that had frequently been the norm.

Independent institutions and a full cycle approach

The growth in parliaments' capacity to carry out full-cycle engagement in legislative processes is closely linked to the expansion in number and role of independent institutions that carry out oversight of specific areas such as audit, human rights, corruption, etc. While the specific range of institutions, responsibilities, and institutional accountability differs from country to country, in most democracies, several of the core independent institutions are effectively parliamentary in nature; members being appointed by parliament, and the primary recipient of reports also being parliament.

Independent institutions have dedicated expertise, and budgets, enabling them to carry out rigorous assessment of the overall situation and specific issues of concern in their mandate area. While for example, a Finance Committee of parliament may have only a handful of staff, an Auditor General's Office could have over one hundred professional public auditors. Thus, the depth and focus of work are exponentially greater than parliament itself could hope to achieve. Further, most independent institutions not only prepare annual reports, but also carry out special investigations on issues of particular concern; typically, parliament is empowered to request special reports from independent oversight institutions as needed.

Parliaments of course need to be able to make use of independent institutions' work. In some emerging democracies, parliament and particularly parliamentary committees may have no track record of carrying out useful oversight, and in previous authoritarian regimes, whatever quasi-independent oversight institutions might have existed, would likely have reported to the head of state or the government. Capacity building, including through external support, is therefore frequently required to build oversight awareness and capacities so that parliament can make use of independent institution reports. The most important feature of parliament's use of independent institution reports is through follow-up that ensures that government responds to adopted recommendations for reform; reporting back to parliament on what actions it has taken, and explaining whenever government feels that actions could not or should not be taken.

Transnational governance and national parliaments

The growing role of parliament in governance has occurred at the same time as an increasing technicity and outcome orientation in governance. Outcomes of quite complex government programming are increasingly expected to be measurable, and various international governance institutions have taken on the role of international norm setters, ranging from the international financial institutions in the area of PFM,[14] OECD in governance standards (OECD, 2018), with the EU as the first transnational body accruing state-like powers, again based largely on norm-setting rather than physical domination of territory (Djelic & Sahlin-Andersson, 2006). Norm-setting within the parliamentary world is relatively less prescriptive, and the benchmarks that have been developed tend to emphasise the expansion of autonomy and responsibilities rather than prescribing particular organisational models.

The result has been a paradoxical situation in which parliaments are increasingly open, inclusive, and deliberative, while the scope for international diversity in policy development appears to be shrinking. Although the sharing of effective practices is, of course, positive, the circumstances are so different from country to country that governance policy models can rarely simply be transposed. This can create a difficult situation in which parliament is caught between citizens' expectations and a government's international commitments.

Limits to parliamentary engagement in full-cycle governance

Expanded parliamentary engagement throughout the policy cycle is a positive development, in principle. By ensuring parliamentary awareness and input at each stage of policy and regulation development and implementation, the quality of parliamentary engagement will be enhanced, and lessons learned both in reviewing and revising existing policies and regulations, and also for future policy processes. At the same time, there are two significant issues that should be considered as parliament takes on these new roles and responsibilities.

The first is that engagement in the full policy cycle should not disturb the separation of powers between the different arms of the state (primarily, the legislature, the executive, and the judiciary). There are good reasons why the concept of the separation of powers has become a principle of modern democratic government. Montesquieu warned presciently:

> In every government there are three sorts of power: the legislative; the executive in respect to things dependent on the law of nations; and the judiciary in regard to matters that depend on the civil law ... .

> When the legislative and executive powers are united in the same person, or in the same body of magistrates, there can be no liberty; because apprehensions may arise, lest the same monarch or senate should enact tyrannical laws, to execute them in a tyrannical manner ...

> There would be an end of every thing, were the same man, or the same body, whether of the nobles or of the people, to exercise those three powers, that of enacting laws, that of executing the public resolutions, and of trying the causes of individuals. (De Montesquieu, [1748] 1989)

The risk of tyranny caused through the fusion of different branches of the state – inevitably under the dominance of the executive – has been seen countless times since Montesquieu; in the contemporary era, most notably in the authoritarianism of the Soviet system.

The authoritarian risk is not a likely contemporary outcome of parliaments accruing too many powers to themselves; a more likely result is confusion in responsibilities, particularly on the part of citizens. This is seen frequently, for example, where parliaments establish 'constituency development funds' that MPs can use in order to allocate funds to projects in their constituency. Not only does this provide risks of corruption and lack of accountability, but it also leads to citizens believing that MPs are part of the executive, in other words, responsible for implementing government programmes (van Zyl, 2010). Ultimately, this will result in even greater pressure on MPs to promise to deliver services that are actually the remit of the executive. By promising, and then failing to succeed in 'delivering' government services, the reputation of MPs and parliament suffers further decline.

In the fields of parliamentary scrutiny and oversight, particularly through independent institutions, parliament and independent parliamentary institutions can sometimes stray into a quasi-judicial role. Some human rights commissions, for example, have both investigatory and administrative justice powers. While this is not necessarily a problem, use of such powers by independent institutions should be practised entirely independent of parliament to avoid any perception of political interference, and should also be subject to judicial review. Parliament's relationship with independent institutions should be based on broader questions of how state systems function, drawn from annual reports and special reports of the institution as presented to parliament, in addition to regular appearances of the independent institution before the relevant sectoral committee of parliament.

A second and perhaps more practical and universal concern about greater parliamentary engagement through the legislative cycle relates to parliament's practical ability to carry out additional functions. In the emerging democracy context, in particular, parliamentary resources are often scarce; one, or sometimes two staff per committee, limited if any library and research services, legal advisors, etc. Parliament may be struggling to cope with its current work, let alone take on any additional responsibilities.

Often, the organisation and coordination of tasks is a major issue. Many parliaments in emerging democracies lack effective coordination systems and this reduces potential for positive synergies, for example between committee staff, research services, and central administration. However, even with the best possible management systems, there may well be insufficient professional staff in total to effectively take on large new responsibilities. While external support from parliamentary strengthening programmes can sometimes be helpful in building capacity and enhancing services, this must be integrated into the day-to-day functioning of the institution, and with a clear sustainability strategy in place. Otherwise, once the external support ends, and if the additional products, such as regulatory impact assessment and post-legislative scrutiny reports – made possible through the support programme – cease to be produced, the image of parliament can actually decline further, having created a demand for a new product and then failing to continue producing it.

Therefore, both parliaments themselves, and parliamentary strengthening programmes, need to plan carefully, prior to committing to new functions inherent in the full cycle legislative approach. New work responsibilities are best incorporated in overall institutional plans that in turn are tied to internal budget allocation, so that resources required are identified and allocated. Failure to make adequate resource allocation for new responsibilities is one of the most common causes of reform failure in parliaments.

Three case studies

The article now turns to explore three case studies of parliaments (Republic of Georgia, South Africa, and Scotland) that have been innovative in expanding their work beyond the traditional roles of parliament, considering some of the successes and challenges encountered.

Case study – Georgia

Georgia has been the most ambitious of the post-Soviet republics in introducing democratic innovations, notably through parliament, which has become one of the more pioneering in the world. Georgia's parliament is an acknowledged leader in the parliamentary openness movement, hosting several international conferences on parliamentary and governance openness. In 2017, Georgia adopted constitutional changes that transformed the country from a semi-presidential to a parliamentary republic. The powers of the president were substantially reduced, and the president will now be elected through an electoral college comprised of parliamentarians and local government representatives rather than by direct popular vote.

Georgia has taken the lead in extending parliamentary engagement in the legislative – and the overall governance – cycle. Changes to parliament's rules of procedure adopted in 2018 introduced a number of innovations that move the Georgian parliament towards full cycle engagement. These innovations include:

- Enhanced legislative scrutiny tools. Changes in the law governing the requirements for legislation submitted by government to parliament require in most cases the inclusion of regulatory impact assessments, giving parliament tools not only for pre-adoption scrutiny but also a framework for post-legislative scrutiny;

- Expanded oversight tools, including annual reporting to parliament by the prime minister which is followed by parliamentary debate, and can be put to a vote, regular sectoral reports to parliament, and at least annual appearance of ministers before parliament;
- The establishment of a standing audit working group within the Budget and Finance responsible to 'review, evaluate, and make recommendations' on the State Audit Office (SAI) annual and special reports;
- Clarification and simplification of the processes for setting up investigative committees, and for voting no-confidence in the government.

The majority of new provisions in the Rules of Procedure came into effect at the beginning of 2019. It is thus early to assess how effectively these provisions will be implemented. One issue is that the adoption of new and additional responsibilities and processes was not directly linked to assessment of institutional resource implications and capacity of the current parliamentary secretariat to support such changes, or to revisions in budgetary and human resource allocations. Therefore, it will be important to monitor in practice how effectively the new parliamentary responsibilities are implemented. Another factor important to success will be the institutionalisation of the Georgian parliament's extended roles, which to date have been driven, and to some extent implemented, primarily by reformers in important leadership roles in parliament. It is not clear what will happen if the individuals driving reform no longer hold key positions (Civil Georgia, 2019).

Case study – South Africa

After the end of apartheid and with the crafting of a new constitution that was adopted in 1997, South Africa set out to be an innovator in parliamentary processes, particularly through institutionalised opportunities for citizen participation, and through the establishment of a category of independent institutions, so-called Chapter Nine institutions,[15] that provide oversight of government and also support parliamentary oversight of the executive, and follow up of oversight enquiries and initiatives.

These Chapter Nine institutions are the Public Protector, the South African Human Rights Commission (SAHRC), the Commission for the Promotion and Protection of the Rights of Cultural, Religious and Linguistic Communities (CRL Rights Commission), the Commission for Gender Equality (CGE), the Auditor-General, and the Independent Electoral Commission (IEC). As the Constitution notes, 'These institutions are accountable to the National Assembly, and must report on their activities and the performance of their functions to the Assembly at least once a year'. All the members of the different independent commissions are appointed by parliament, on the basis that they should be representative of South Africa's diverse ethnic communities, as well as assuring gender equality. Members of the commissions must be approved by an absolute majority of the total number of MPs; in the case of the Public Protector, by at least 60 per cent of all MPs.

The South African constitution also emphasises the importance of public participation in parliament's work. In particular, it mandates that parliament must receive petitions, encourage public involvement in legislative and other processes, and conduct business openly and transparently. Beyond the constitutional framework, the South African Legislative Sector (SALS), an informal grouping of the country's national and provincial legislatures, has established a 'Framework for Public Participation', finalised in 2013 (South Africa Legislative Sector, 2013; Waterhouse, 2015). The Framework, built on both the constitutional and legal framework in South Africa, and on best practice models for public participation – many of which originated in South Africa – provides a highly structured, step-by-step approach to the various tools and avenues for citizen engagement across national and provincial assemblies.

One continuing issue in the strengthening of the South African parliament has been the relative dominance of one political party. This has sometimes meant that, while progressive accountability procedures are well-articulated in the constitution, the dominant majority party has in practice been able to limit the scope of effective scrutiny (de Vos, 2012; HopolangSelebalo, 2011). At the same time, the balance of forces within parliament has become increasingly more even in recent years, and the opposition has been able to raise key issues and focus attention, often successfully, on the need for enhanced accountability and political reform.

Case study – Scotland

From its inception in 1999, the modern Scottish Parliament has been an innovator. Although it is a subnational institution, with certain powers still reserved to the Westminster parliament and government, Scotland's parliament has consistently sought both to extend its powers and mandate, and to establish a full cycle approach to engagement in the governance process.

After a referendum of Scottish citizens on governance devolution in 1997, in which almost three-quarters of voters approved the reestablishment of a Scottish parliament, a major consultative process was undertaken in order to establish the priorities of Scottish citizens for their new parliament. The initial report summarised the input received:

> our recommendations envisage an open, accessible Parliament; a Parliament where power is shared with the people; where people are encouraged to participate in the policy making process which affects all our lives; an accountable, visible Parliament; and a Parliament which promotes equal opportunities for all.[16]

The Scottish parliament has focused considerable attention on post-legislative scrutiny. Interestingly, the parliamentary committee that addresses PLS is also responsible for audit; a choice that means that PLS is the specific responsibility of one committee rather than all sectoral committees. The Audit and PLS committee is particularly diligent in carrying out its work, and in common with the tradition for Public Accounts Committees in Commonwealth countries, it is chaired ('convened') by a member of the political opposition.

The main stress is also placed on public participation. Each session, a participation strategy with objectives is drawn up. For the January 2018 session, for example, the following priorities were identified, each with an action strategy:

- 'Implement engagement recommendations from Commission on Parliamentary Reform
- Effective public participation in the work of the Parliament [issues-based engagement]
- Improving awareness of the relevance and accessibility of the Parliament, particularly in under-represented groups
- Staff with the capacity, knowledge and skills to meet changing needs and expectations'[17]

At any one time, the Scottish parliament is engaged with a variety of different consultations.[18] These can be in relation to draft legislation that has been submitted to parliament and referred to a committee for scrutiny – in April 2019 a consultation was being carried out by the local government committee on local business taxes; it can be in relation to individual members' bills – in April 2019, 7 pieces of private member's draft legislation were out for consultation; or it can involve a broader issue of public concern where a parliamentary committee wishes to understand the issue and develop recommendations for possible government implementation. For example, again in April 2019, the parliament was requesting public input on the issue of empty homes in Scotland, on the future of primary health care, on housing subsidies, and on health hazards in the health care industry.

New parliamentary engagements – challenges and opportunities

In the next section, we will look at some specific opportunities and challenges in the different expanding areas of parliamentary work, from pre-legislative consultations to regulatory impact assessments, to post-legislative scrutiny.

Pre-legislative consultations

Westminster-model parliaments and governments have followed the practice of publishing Green and White Papers for many years. While Green Papers traditionally contain a number of policy options, White Papers propose a single pathway and argue for the type of policy initiative that the government would like to put into law. Thus, input is encouraged at earlier or later stages of policy development. There has been pressure for emerging country parliaments, even from different constitutional traditions, to adopt the same practice. The advantage of such an approach is that, for major pieces of legislation, public and interest group concerns can be addressed and incorporated where possible in the draft legislation. The approach can build support for policy intervention on a consensual basis.

Governments sometimes resist an excess of early consultation on the basis that they can lose control of the policy process and end up being pressured into accepting legislation that is far from their policy goal, and which may be inconsistent with the broader direction of government policy; for example, policy inputs from the public may often have a price-tag attached, but government operates within a tight fiscal framework and may not be willing, or in the case of countries dependent on foreign donors, even able to invest more resources into a particular area.

In some jurisdictions, such as Scotland, the practice is mainly to hold consultations on specific pieces of legislation that have already been tabled by government or an individual member, or on broad policy issues, rather than specifically in the Green Paper or White Paper format.

Regulatory impact assessments

Regulatory Impact Assessments (RIA) emerged in the 1990s, initially primarily as a means to ensure that government was not simply continuously adding to the regulatory burden on citizens and businesses. The objective was to require government to clearly articulate how the regulation would impact the economy and society, and also determine if there were ways to achieve the same goals, and whether legislation could be combined or repealed. The basic analytical principles for RIA are that regulation should be assessed in terms of whether it is *proportional, accountable, consistent, transparent,* and *targeted*. Since the emergence of RIAs, they have become less focused on the idea of 'bonfire of regulation' that was popular in the Margaret Thatcher era, and often simply entail a thorough examination of overall impact. In the UK system, RIAs, carried out within government, are obligatory for most new legislation. Evidently, RIA is a useful tool for parliament as it provides a solid basis for legislative scrutiny. RIA can also be useful in Post-Legislative Scrutiny as it contains a statement of what government expected would be the impact.

In order for parliaments to make good use of RIAs, they must have the capacity to effectively and critically analyse these documents. Given that the RIA is reviewing the impact of a piece of legislation being proposed by government, it can be anticipated that while truthful, the government's RIA will tend to emphasise a positive impact scenario. Thus, parliamentary staff and parliamentarians will benefit from training in effective RIA analysis.

One emergent risk in parliamentary involvement in RIAs is that in some cases, parliaments have been encouraged, by donors and parliamentary support actors, to themselves carry out quite thorough RIAs, typically with external support.[19] While there might be justifications for such an approach in very specific circumstances, in general for parliaments to carry out full RIAs rather than carefully reviewing ones prepared by government represents an overreach of parliament's role; technical analyses are properly the responsibility of the executive rather than parliament.

Post-legislative scrutiny

Post-Legislative Scrutiny is another expanding area of parliamentary work. The logic of PLS is clear; if parliament is to pass legislation, it should also assess whether that legislation has been implemented, and what issues have arisen. The movement to institutionalise and expand PLS has been driven particularly from the Westminster parliament, with Lord Norton of Louth playing a key role. It has then been integrated into parliamentary development work, with the Westminster Foundation for Democracy taking a leadership role. Although PLS is best known through studies on Westminster-type parliaments, various forms of PLS exist in numerous non-Westminster parliaments. There are still divergences regarding the appropriate focus of PLS; should it be mainly a technical assessment of legislative implementation as in France, or a broader assessment of legislative impact, as in Scotland, for example?

Conclusion

The article has traced a gradual enlargement of parliaments' roles in the policy cycle, towards what I describe as full-cycle engagement in governance. This expansion of parliamentary purview has been driven to a large extent by growing citizen expectations, in turn, fostered through a mutually-reinforcing cycle of instantaneous communication and enforced institutional transparency. Further, the policy-making environment has become more competitive. This has occurred both through the increased technicity of decision-making and the growth of expert-driven norm-setting, and through competition for legitimacy from practitioners of participatory and associative democracy. Parliaments have had to justify their relevance and conform to pressure to demonstrate effectiveness.

The article has described a range of new or expanded roles that parliaments are playing, as they move towards a 'watertight' approach in which they engage in each step of the public policy process from conception to scrutiny, to enactment, monitoring and evaluation. The logic for parliaments to be involved throughout the legislative development, implementation and post-legislative scrutiny phases is irrefutable. This full-cycle engagement breaks through a silo approach in which actors are responsible only for their particular piece of the policy cycle, without giving consideration to the overall process and its outcomes.

As noted, however, there are some risks; which include the danger that parliament exceeds its mandate and starts carrying out technical work that is best done by government experts. The representation function of parliament is carried out most effectively when it is at the level of policy principles and drawing conclusions based on technical expertise, rather than attempting to substitute for that expertise. Taking these new or expanded roles, in turn, some of the challenges to be addressed in expanded parliamentary engagement are as follows.

In institutionalising parliament's role in *pre-legislative consultations*, agreement must be reached with governments on if and how parliament should take on the consultative role? In many countries, governments prefer to manage such processes themselves, based on their greater access to policy expertise. For parliamentary pre-legislative consultations to be effective, government will need to be prepared and able to produce Green Paper / White Paper or legislative discussion notes.

Further, parliaments will need to establish procedures for organising consultative processes. This requires adequate parliamentary resources to carry out consultations, especially if regional hearings are to be conducted. In particular, sufficient parliamentary human resources are needed with capacities for effective communications of hearings, support during the consultation process, and timely reporting of consultation results. Failure to adequately publicise and ensure citizen and expert engagement will render even the most important consultative exercise a failure.

Parliaments around the world are increasingly engaged with Regulatory Impact Assessments (RIA) as part of the legislative scrutiny process. Again, parliaments' technical expertise to conduct such assessments may be limited, and providing that government RIA is trusted to be neutral and expert-driven, parliaments may be better suited to scrutinising the results of RIAs rather than carrying them out themselves.

In many countries, MP-initiated legislative proposals are not subject to government RIA, in which case parliament needs to ensure due diligence is carried out on potential impacts. This is particularly important in countries where parliament-initiated legislation is a substantial proportion of overall legislative work.

For members of the EU, candidate members, and countries in associative relationships with the EU, EU legislation harmonisation and transposition can be a particular challenge. Frequently, governments may not carry out thorough RIA of such legislation, and will ask parliament to routinely adopt it. This can be a controversial issue because EU association and accession agreements tend to be unidirectional – the associate or candidate country agrees to adopt European acquis. However, effective parliamentary RIA is crucial in pointing out impact on particular sectors of the national economy, providing the possibility for amelioration measures.

For effective financial and programme oversight and audit, parliaments require the support of strong independent institutions. These institutions include the Supreme Audit Institution, but increasingly also other independent institutions such as human rights commissions, ombudspersons, privacy and transparency commissioners, etc.

In emerging democracies, there is often little history of effective oversight, and both staff and MPs may require capacity development – also, oversight needs to be built into committee work plans. For the process to be effective, oversight recommendations need to be followed up. As discussed above, this is frequently the weak point in parliamentary oversight in general, and particularly in relation to independent oversight institutions. If parliamentarians are not really engaged in the work of the independent institutions (and sometimes not even supportive), then there is a high likelihood that reports will be received by parliament without a great deal of attention, and without a real expectation of government responses.

Post-Legislative scrutiny can be carried out in a number of different ways, and at different levels of detail. This determines whether parliament carries out PLS for all legislation (in which case a light touch approach of formal compliance should be chosen), or if, instead, more in-depth analysis of a selected number of key pieces of legislation is to be carried out.

Where PLS extends beyond a formal assessment of legislative implementation (for example scrutiny of if the law has been proclaimed and if required regulations adopted), then a system for selecting legislation for PLS needs to be established. Where PLS is mainly focused on assuring that all the necessary formal implementation steps have been taken; as is the case in France, it may be appropriate to centralise the PLS function in the parliamentary administration, or in the legislation committee or equivalent; otherwise, PLS should be carried out by the same sectoral committee to which the draft legislation was originally referred for scrutiny, assuring knowledgeable and consistent scrutiny.

PLS can be supported by a special administrative unit (such as in Westminster, the Scrutiny Unit), or by parliamentary committee staff; in any case, PLS expansion has human resource implications for parliaments and needs to be budgeted. In countries with an upper house, this may be an appropriate location for carrying out in-depth PLS. Whereas in more highly politicised lower houses, there may be an attempt to 'relitigate' the underlying principles of legislation, which is generally not appropriate in PLS, upper houses will often take a more dispassionate view, focusing primarily on the anticipated and unanticipated consequences of the legislation, and considering ways legislation could be improved, as well as taking broader lessons for future legislative development.

Notes

1. An earlier version of this paper was presented at the Westminster Foundation for Democracy expert seminar, Legislative impact assessments and Post-Legislative Scrutiny, London, 26 April 2019.
2. Parties themselves are widely seen as being in crisis, especially in terms of their capacity to accumulate and represent citizen perspectives, see for example, Conti et al. (2018).
3. Peter Dominiczak Theresa May to dare Parliament to 'defy the will of the people' if she loses Article 50 court battle, 3 Decenber 2016, *Daily Telegraph* (UK). https://www.telegraph.co.uk/news/2016/12/02/theresa-may-dare-parliament-defy-will-people-loses-article-50/.
4. The various contemporary challenges to post World War II mainstream politics in numerous countries have often been grouped together and described as populism. The definition of populism is a subject of extensive debate; I adopt that of Mansfield and Macedo (59) as having a, 'common conceptual core: the "people" in a moral battle against "elites"'. Parliaments and parliamentarians are routinely included within the 'Elite Other' within populist discourse, see Mansbridge and Macedo (2019).
5. The trope of parliamentary irresponsibility is evoked recurrently in critiques of representative democracy, and has justified numerous movements to assert executive domination (e.g., Lindseth, 2003).
6. De Vrieze (2019, p. 5) uses this definition, '[i]ndependent oversight institutions exercise oversight over the democratic functioning and integrity of the executive and state administration'. Although there is a plethora of forms of autonomy and independence, these typically include i9ndependence of functioning and protection from retaliation from the state bodies the institution oversees. In many cases, independent oversight institutions report to parliament (see Murphy & De Vrieze, 2020).
7. Data accessed at http://siteresourcesworldbank.org/PUBLICSECTORAND GOVERNANCE/Resources/285741-1233946247437/5810405-1399294268994/ Ombudsman-presentation.pdf.
8. In 1999, the author collaborated with the late Canadian Member of Parliament Reg Alcock in his efforts to dialogue with citizens; Mr. Alcock advised that a primary motivation was to wrest legitimacy from civil society organisations. In November 2005, the author was involved in organising a consultation between parliamentarians and civil society representatives at the National Assembly of Burkina Faso in Ouagadougou on Parliament's ten year strategic plan; when civil society representatives started to criticise the performance of MPs and the parliament, the MPs left the room, one stating that 'we were

elected by thousands of citizens; you elected yourselves' (see also, Bouwen, 2007, p. 275; Lang, 2012, p. x).
9. http://www.democraticaudit.com/2018/03/02/a-citizens-convention-for-uk-democracy-is-more-necessary-with-every-passing-day/.
10. https://www.theguardian.com/world/2010/feb/25/nigel-farage-herman-van-rompuy-damp-rag.
11. https://www.indy100.com/article/brexit-nigel-farage-european-parliament-mep-esther-de-lange-video-8822271.
12. See for example, https://www.oireachtas.ie/en/visit-and-learn/teachers-and-students/.
13. See for example, https://www.parliament.scot/visitandlearn/109327.aspx.
14. See the Public Expenditure Framework Assessment, https://www.pefa.org/about.
15. https://www.gov.za/documents/constitution-republic-south-africa-1996-chapter-9-state-institutions-supporting.
16. https://www.parliament.scot/PublicInformationdocuments/Report_of_the_Consultative_Steering_Group.pdf.
17. https://www.parliament.scot/PublicEngagement/PES_2017.pdf.
18. https://www.parliament.scot/gettinginvolved/current-consultations.aspx.
19. See for example, http://www.parliament.ge/en/saparlamento-saqmianoba/komitetebi/evropastan-integraciis-komiteti-143/axali-ambebi1910/momxmareblis-uflebebis-dacvis-shesaxeb-saqartvelos-kanonproeqttan-dakavshirebit-regulirebis-zegavlenis-shefasebis-ria-angarishis-prezentacia-gaimarta.page; and http://www.pmcg-i.com/projects/item/1468-regulatory-impact-assessment-on-options-for-establishment-of-an-employment-mechanism.

Disclosure statement

No potential conflict of interest was reported by the author(s).

References

Assemblée Parlementaire de la Francophonie. (2009). *La réalité démocratique des Parlements: Quels critères d'évaluation?* http://apf.francophonie.org/La-realite-democratique-des.html

Barkan, J. (2005). *Emerging legislature or rubber stamp? The South African national assembly after ten years of democracy.* University of Cape Town, Centre for Social Science Research. http://hdl.handle.net/11427/19368

Beetham, D. (Ed.). (2006). *Parliament and democracy in the twenty-first century: A guide to good practice*. Inter-Parliamentary Union. https://www.ipu.org/resources/publications/handbooks/2016-07/parliament-and-democracy-in-twenty-first-century-guide-good-practice

Bouwen, P. (2007). Competing for consultation: Civil society and conflict between the European Commission and the European parliament. *West European Politics, 30*(2), 265–284. https://doi.org/10.1080/01402380701239715

Brazier, A. (2004). *Issues in law making, 5: Pre-legislative scrutiny*. Hansard Society Briefing Paper.

Burns, T. R. (1999). The evolution of parliaments and societies in Europe. *European Journal of Social Theory, 2*(2), 167–194. https://doi.org/10.1177/13684319922224392

Civil Georgia. (2019, November 14). *Seven Georgian dream MPs leave parliamentary majority, positions*. https://civil.ge/archives/326325

Commonwealth Parliamentary Association. (2018). *Recommended benchmarks for democratic legislatures*. http://www.cpahq.org/cpahq/Main/CPA_Benchmarks/Main/Programmes/Benchmarks_for_democratic_Legislatures.aspx

Conti, N., Hutter, S., & Nanou, K. (2018). Party competition and political representation in crisis: An introductory note. *Party Politics, 24*(1), 3–9. https://doi.org/10.1177/1354068817740758

Cooke, B., & Kothari, U. (Eds.). (2001). *Participation: The new tyranny?* Zed Books.

De Montesquieu, C. ([1748] 1989). *Montesquieu: The spirit of the laws*. Cambridge University Press. Book Six.

de Vos, P. (2012). Balancing independence and accountability: The role of Chapter 9 institutions in South Africa's constitutional democracy. In D. M. Chirwa, & L. Nijzink (Eds.), *Accountable government in Africa: Perspectives from public law and political studies* (pp. 160–177). United Nations University Press.

De Vrieze, F. (2019). *Independent oversight institutions and regulatory agencies, and their relationship to parliament: Outline of assessment framework*. WFD. https://www.wfd.org/wp-content/uploads/2019/02/WEB_INDEPENDENT-OVERSIGHT-INS.pdf

Djelic, M. L., & Sahlin-Andersson, K. (Eds.). (2006). *Transnational governance: Institutional dynamics of regulation*. Cambridge University Press.

Doherty, I. (2001). Democracy out of balance. *Policy Review, 106*, 25–35. https://www.hoover.org/research/democracy-out-balance

Fukuyama, F. (2006). *The end of history and the last man*. Simon and Schuster.

Häkkinen, T. (2014). *The royal prerogative redefined: Parliamentary debate on the role of the British parliament in large-scale military deployments, 1982-2003 (No. 224)*. University of Jyväskylä.

Henman, P. (2016). Performing the state: The socio-political dimensions of performance measurement in policy and public services. *Policy Studies, 37*(6), 499–507. https://doi.org/10.1080/01442872.2016.1144739

HopolangSelebalo. (2011). *Challenges to public participation in South Africa's parliament*. ISS. https://issafrica.org/iss-today/challenges-to-public-participation-in-south-africas-parliament

Johnson, C., & Talbot, C. (2007). The UK parliament and performance. *International Review of Administrative Sciences, 73*(1), 113–131. https://doi.org/10.1177/0020852307075693

Lang, S. (2012). *NGOs, civil society, and the public sphere*. Cambridge University Press.

Lester, A. (2002). Parliamentary scrutiny of legislation under the human rights Act 1998. *Victoria University of Wellington Law Review, 33*(1). https://130.195.21.34/vuwlr/article/download/5853/5188

Leston-Bandeira, C. (2012). Studying the relationship between parliament and citizens. *The Journal of Legislative Studies, 18*(3-4), 265–274. https://doi.org/10.1080/13572334.2012.706044

Lewis, C. (2002). The declining reputation of politicians: Is it deserved? *Australasian Parliamentary Review, 17*(1), 131–144. https://www.aspg.org.au/wp-content/uploads/2017/09/10-Lewis-PolysReputations.pdf

Lienert, M. I. (2010). *Role of the legislature in budget processes*. International Monetary Fund.

Lindseth, P. L. (2003). The paradox of parliamentary supremacy: Delegation, democracy, and dictatorship in Germany and France, 1920s-1950s. *Yale Law Journal, 113*(7), 1341–1415. https://doi.org/10.2307/4135771

Lynch, T. D., & Day, S. E. (1996). Public sector performance measurement. *Public Administration Quarterly, 19*(4), 404–419. https://doi.org/10.2307/41288141

Mansbridge, J., & Macedo, S. (2019). Populism and democratic theory. *Annual Review of Law and Social Science, 15*(1), 59–77. https://doi.org/10.1146/annurev-lawsocsci-101518-042843

Murphy, J., & De Vrieze, F. (2020). *Parliaments and independent oversight institutions*. Westminster Foundation for Democracy. https://www.wfd.org/wp-content/uploads/2020/02/WFD_Publication_IOI_web.pdf

Naidoo, K. (2003, February10). *Civil society, governance and globalisation*. Presented at the World Bank headquarters in Washington. http://www.lasociedadcivil.org/wp-content/uploads/2014/11/naidoo_copy3.pdf

Norton, P. (2019). Post-legislative scrutiny in the UK parliament: Adding value. *The Journal of Legislative Studies, 25*(3), 340–357. https://doi.org/10.1080/13572334.2019.1633778

O'Brien, M., Stapenhurst, R., & Von Trapp, L. (Eds.). (2016). *Benchmarking and self-assessment for parliaments*. The World Bank.

OECD. (2018). *Policy framework on sound public governance*. https://www.oecd.org/governance/policy-framework-on-sound-public-governance/draft-policy-framework-on-sound-public-governance.pdf

Palonen, K. (2016). *The politics of parliamentary procedure: The formation of the Westminster procedure as a parliamentary ideal type*. Verlag Barbara Budrich.

Pap, A. L. (2017). *Democratic decline in Hungary: Law and society in an illiberal democracy*. Routledge.

Power, G. (2012). *Global parliamentary report: The changing nature of parliamentary representation*. Inter-Parliamentary Union.

Radaelli, C. M., & De Francesco, F. (2010). Regulatory impact assessment. In R. Baldwin, M. Cave, & M. Lodge (Eds.), *The Oxford handbook of regulation* (pp. 279–301). Oxford University Press.

SADC Parliamentary Forum. (2010). *Benchmarks for Democratic Legislatures in Southern Africa*. https://agora-parl.org/sites/default/files/sadc_pf_-_benchmarks_for_democratic_legislatures_in_southern_africa.pdf

Scholte, J. A. (2004). Civil society and democratically accountable global governance. *Government and Opposition, 39*(2), 211–233. https://doi.org/10.1111/j.1477-7053.2004.00121.x

South Africa Legislative Sector. (2013). *Public participation framework for the South African legislative Sector*. Parliament of South Africa. https://web.archive.org/web/20180328192118/http://www.sals.gov.za/docs/pubs/ppf.pdf

Tellier, G. (2015). Improving the relevance of parliamentary institutions: An examination of legislative pre-budget consultations in British Columbia. *The Journal of Legislative Studies, 21*(2), 192–212. https://doi.org/10.1080/13572334.2014.953841

Urbinati, N. (2006). *Representative democracy: Principles and genealogy*. University of Chicago Press.

Urbinati, N. (2012). Rousseau on the risks of representing the sovereign. *PolitischeVierteljahresschrift, 53*(4), 646–667. https://doi.org/10.5771/0032-3470-2012-4-646

Urbinati, N. (2016). A pragmatic view of democratic proceduralism. *Global Discourse, 6*(1-2), 227–232. https://doi.org/10.1080/23269995.2015.1104127

van Zyl, A. (2010). *What is wrong with the constituency development funds?* (International Budget Partnership Working Paper 3/10). https://ideas.repec.org/p/ess/wpaper/id2644.html#download

Verbeeten, F. H., & Speklé, R. F. (2015). Management control, results-oriented culture and public sector performance: Empirical evidence on new public management. *Organization Studies, 36*(7), 953–978. https://doi.org/10.1177/0170840615580014

Waterhouse, S. J. (2015). *People's parliament? An assessment of public participation in South Africa's legislatures* [Doctoral dissertation, University of Cape Town]. https://open.uct.ac.za/bitstream/handle/11427/15198/thesis_law_2015_waterhouse_samantha_jane.pdf;sequence=1

Wehner, J. (2010). Institutional constraints on profligate politicians: The conditional effect of partisan fragmentation on budget deficits. *Comparative Political Studies, 43*(2), 208–229. https://doi.org/10.1177/0010414009347828

Whitmore, C. (2019, July 17). *Supreme betrayal: What Ukrainians think about their parliament*. Vox Ukraine. https://voxukraine.org/en/supreme-betrayer-what-ukrainians-think-about-their-parliament/

Index

active ex-post evaluation 58, 74
activist parliaments 122–123
Act of Parliament 2, 40, 94, 111
ad hoc committees 40–41, 43, 61, 91, 93
Australia 9–10, 14–15, 17–18, 20–25,
　27–29, 31, 111
Australian Human Rights Commission
　(AHRC) 23–24, 26
Australian Law Reform Commission
　(ALRC) 23–24
Australian model of legislative review 32
Australian Parliament 14, 20, 22–23

Bates, S. 41
Boulding, K. 51
Brazier, A. 41
Bulgaria 58
Bundestag 85

Caygill, T. 91–92
citizens 9, 15, 19, 31, 64, 121, 123–124,
　126–129, 131–132, 137, 139
citizenship 69, 72–73
citizenship by investment (CBI) 72–73
civil society 113, 121, 124
Coalition Government 44, 46, 54
coalition legislation 49, 51
committee reports 62, 64, 67, 73, 88
committee work programmes 50–51, 54
Commons Education Committee 51, 53
Commonwealth Parliamentary
　Association 125
community engagement 9, 20, 29–32
constitutional affairs 21, 24–25, 66
Constitution Committee 3, 5–7
control committees 94–95
core tasks 40–41
cross-border divisions 69–70
cross-border mergers 59, 69–70
culture 31, 40, 42–43, 47, 66

Datta, S. K. 101
dedicated legislation 6, 105
deliberative approach 14, 19, 29, 31–32
deliberative decision-making 20
deliberative law making 19
democracy 7, 11, 15–16, 102, 110, 123,
　125–127, 130, 138
democratic competition 124
De Montesquieu, C. 131–132
De Vrieze, F. 39
draft legislation 136–137, 140
dual mechanism 61

Equality Act 47
European Implementation Assessment
　(EIA) 61–68
European Parliament 57–59, 61, 63–65,
　67–70, 72, 74–75, 128
European Parliamentary Research Service
　(EPRS) 61
European Parliament evaluations 65
evaluation process 8, 88, 95
ex-post evaluation 57–63, 67, 71, 74–75,
　86, 90
ex-post scrutiny 59, 86
extra-parliamentary bodies 17

federal laws 23–24, 29, 32, 84
financial legislation 48
Fitsilis, F. 6, 9
formal scrutinisers 81, 83–84, 88, 90, 96
formal scrutiny 60–61
Fox, R. 41
France 58, 60, 80, 84, 87–88, 90, 96, 138, 140
French National Assembly 89–90
Fukuyama, F. 126

Geddes, M. 50, 52–53
gender 19, 25, 27–28, 112
Georgia 113, 122, 133

INDEX

Germany 80, 84, 96
golden visas 59, 68–69, 72
governance process 121, 127, 135
governmental documents 87–88
government departments 10, 15–16, 39, 42, 44, 46, 48–51, 54, 91, 103
Griglio, E. 81

Hansard Society 40, 52
Hasson, V. 39
Home Affairs Committee 48
House of Commons 4, 7, 16, 39–40, 43, 47–48, 54, 61, 91–92, 103
House of Commons Education Committee 51, 53
House of Lords 3, 7, 40–43, 46–47, 61, 91–93
Houses of Parliament 17, 20–21, 54, 90, 92

inclusive institutions 101, 103
independent institutions 121, 130, 132, 134, 140
independent scrutinisers 81, 83–84, 93, 95–96
individual rights 15, 21–23
Indonesia 16, 113
informal scrutinisers 81–83, 87, 96
informal scrutiny 60–62, 74
Inter-Parliamentary Union (IPU) 6, 104–105, 115
Italy 58, 60, 80, 84, 86, 96, 103

LCA Committee 25–27
LCA Legislation Committee 28
legislative amendments 25–26
legislative cycle 51, 54, 64–65, 122–123, 132
legislative evaluation 8, 93, 95, 113
legislative proposals 59, 68, 71, 123
legislative scrutiny 14–15, 17–18, 20, 22, 24, 29, 32, 83, 87, 122, 127
legislatures 2, 4–7, 10–11, 62, 74, 105–106, 121–122, 131
Licensing Act 46–47
Lisbon Treaty 59
Lukes, S. 51

Marriage Act 9, 15, 18, 24, 27
Millennium Development Goals (MDGs) 101–102
Moulds, S. 9
multi-committee scrutiny 27
Murphy, Jonathan 6

national parliaments 130
National Regulatory Reform Council (NKR) 85

Palonen, Kari 126
parent legislation 111
parliamentarians 10–11, 25, 31, 87, 123–124, 129, 133, 138, 140
parliamentary committees 3, 6, 16–17, 19, 21, 23, 27–29, 32, 40–41, 44, 60–61, 85, 87–88, 94–95, 136
Parliamentary Control of the Administration (PCA) 94–95
parliamentary engagement 11, 15, 122–123, 131–132
parliamentary involvement 101, 105–108, 114, 116, 123, 138
parliamentary processes 69, 121, 134
parliamentary scrutiny 21, 29, 115, 132
parliaments, categorisation of 80
passive scrutinisers 81–82, 85, 96
plebiscites 30, 128
policy cycle 57–59, 64–65, 68–69, 123, 125, 128, 131, 138–139
policy learning 58, 64, 71, 75
political report/resolution 61
political will 10
populism 122, 129
populist challenge 128
post-enactment scrutiny 22
post-legislative gap 7, 40, 46–47, 50
post-legislative review 8–9, 44, 46, 49–51, 54
powers 19, 21–23, 25–26, 41, 51, 59, 61, 123, 125–126, 131–133, 135
pre-legislative consultations 122, 136–137, 139
primary legislation 111
procedimentalisation 84, 91
public inquiries 20–21, 23, 30
public participation 135–136
public policies 86–87, 89

Rabbany, H. 101
regulatory impact assessment (RIA) 85, 137–140
representative democracy 122–126
research capacities 87–88
residency by investment (RBI) schemes 72–73
resource constraints 10
review clauses 23, 64, 80, 85

review process 23–24
rights scrutiny 31
Riksdag 87–88
Russell, M. 42

SADC Parliamentary Forum 125
Scotland 112, 122, 129, 133, 135–138
scrutiny 3–7, 9, 11, 15–16, 21–22, 24, 40, 42, 48, 51–53, 87–88, 90–91, 136, 139–140
secondary legislation 5–6, 80, 111, 115
sectoral committees 58, 90, 136, 140
senate 21–22, 25, 60, 86, 89–90, 131
Senate Standing Committee 21, 24–25
separation of powers 131
Sex Discrimination Act (SDA) 9, 15, 24–27
South Africa 28, 113, 122, 133–135
special committee 63, 68–69, 72, 74, 114
Special Committee on Financial Crimes 68, 72
stakeholders 5, 64, 70–71, 91, 96, 106, 113, 116
standing committees 60–61, 63, 65–66, 88–89
Statute Law Review 17
statutory legislation 87–88
sunset clauses 22, 29, 80
sustainable development 85, 100–103, 105, 114
sustainable development goals (SDGs) 6, 19, 100–112, 114–115
Sweden 28, 58, 60–61, 80, 84, 87–88, 96
Swiss parliaments 95

Switzerland 80, 84, 93, 95–96, 113
systematic approaches 10, 15–16, 18, 20, 22, 24, 33, 39–40, 91
systematic post-legislative scrutiny 4, 43, 52

tax evasion 63, 68, 72–74
temporary committees 63, 65, 67–68
thematic committees 6, 112
Three Faces of Power 51
time period 23, 44, 46, 49
transnational governance 130
transparency 58, 64, 67, 74, 84, 129
turnover 41, 53–54
turnover of committee membership 53–54

United Kingdom (UK) 2, 4, 6–8, 10–11, 14–17, 20–21, 39–40, 58, 60, 91, 96, 111, 113
United Nations 6, 100, 102, 104
upper Houses 84, 86, 140–141
Urbinati, Nadia 126

variable 80–81
Voluntary National Reviews (VNRs) 106–107, 116

waterhouse 135
Westminster Foundation 7, 11, 15–16, 102, 110, 138
Westminster Foundation for Democracy (WFD) 7, 11, 15–16, 18–19, 102, 110
women 26, 52, 103, 112